Powerful Places in Brittany

Powerful Places in Brittany

Elyn Aviva &
Gary White

Powerful Places in Brittany

by

Elyn Aviva & Gary White

ISBN: 978-0-9826233-2-9

Library of Congress Control Number:

2010936031

Set in Adobe Caslon Pro 11 pt. and Briso Pro 11 pt., with display in Adobe Caslon Pro in various sizes. Cover and title set in Reliq Std and Briso Pro

Cover photo: Chêne des Hindrés, photo by Elyn Aviva (see p. 127 for description)

Contents

Northwestern Brittany (Finistère)

Eastern Brittany (Ille-et-Vilaine and Morbihan)

Acknowledgments

Gratitude to our mentors and teachers, including Ferran Blasco, Mara Freeman, Juan Li, Sig Lonegren, Anne Parker, R. J. Stewart, and Dominique Susani. Gratitude to all the earth-mystery writers and researchers, including Paul Devereux, Tom Graves, and Nigel Pennick, who have opened the way for so many others. Gratitude to our friends for their comments and corrections. Gratitude to each other for patience, tolerance, enthusiasm, and inspiration. Gratitude to the land, the stones, the trees, the temples. For those interested in following up with our teachers we offer the following websites:

Ferran Blasco: http://www.zahoriart.com/

Mara Freeman: http://www.chalicecentre.net/

Juan Li: http://www.ichingdao.org/tao/en/biography-of-juan-li.html

Sig Lonegren: http://www.geomancy.org/

Anne Parker: http://latitudewithattitude.com/

R. J. Stewart: http://www.rjstewart.org/

Dominique Susani: http://sacredgeometryarts.com/

Introduction to Powerful Places

Over the years we have traveled to a number of unusual places, drawn by curiosity, lured by possibility. Gradually we realized that although many of these sites were interesting, some of them were really powerful. These were places where we felt something out of the ordinary—ranging from a shiver up the spine to an unexpected sense of serenity to a strong intimation that we had entered a "thin place" where the veil between this world and the "other realm" was more easily parted.

What we experienced in these places was an interaction between the energies of the place itself, the human activities at that location (offerings, ceremonies, constructions such as stone circles or temples), and our own openness to experience what was happening at that moment. The feeling that a particular place is powerful can take many forms, and it can be subtle or very strong.

In this guidebook we describe some of the more powerful places we have found in Brittany and invite you to experience them for yourself. We make no claims as to what you may or may not feel when visiting these sites. We have observed that one person may bask in the energy of a particular site, another may feel nothing at all, and a third may want to leave as quickly as possible.

On one visit inside a large, earth-covered passage grave in Ireland, Elyn felt increasingly uncomfortable and shaky but (against her better judgment) stayed to listen to our guide. Afterwards, Elyn took a survey and discovered that several people had left immediately because they felt so ill at ease—and others thought the cairn was a wonderful place in which to meditate. In an isolated monastery in the mountains of Spain, we were shown into an abandoned chapel. Instantly, we both felt an incredibly unconditional loving presence. Our companion (a very sensitive and intuitive lady) looked at us in puzzlement. She thought the energy in the room was nothing special.

Our experiences have differed on subsequent visits to the same site. Sometimes the explanation is simple—a large, noisy tour group has just trampled through the site, oblivious to what was there. Other times the answer isn't so obvious. Experiences can never be repeated—whether it's your first taste of a chocolate gelato cone on a sunny day in Rome, or your first kiss, or your first visit to the Grand Canyon. As the Greek philosopher Heraclitus said, "No man ever steps in the same river twice, for it's not the same river and he's not the same man." This is equally true of powerful places.

What makes a place powerful?

The brief answer to "what" is: the land itself has underground water lines, faults or cracks in the earth (sometimes called fire lines), energy vortices, "blind" springs, and so on that our ancestors were able to sense and utilize. An old Gaulish word, *wouivre*, refers to snakes that glide, to rivers that snake through the landscape, and to telluric currents that snake underground from the depths of the terrestrial strata. Experienced dowsers using dowsing rods or pendulums can locate these underground features with great accuracy. If they couldn't, oil exploration and well-digging companies wouldn't waste their money on hiring them.

Our ancestors utilized these energies—and their knowledge of geometry (circles, triangles, pyramid shapes, etc.)—to construct sacred places. For example, an alignment of standing stones may have been placed to draw off energy from an underground fault; a circle of stones may have been built to utilize the energy of an underground spring. The altar of a twelfth-century church may have been carefully placed over the crossing of underground water and fire lines.

"We don't understand how owsing works, but we do unerstand that it can be worked produce usable results, and e also understand how it can worked. In that sense dowsg can be said to be a technolgy, though it can't be scientific." om Graves, *Needles of Stone Resited*, p. 22.

How do you sense these energies?

The brief answer to how to sense these energies is: by centering, grounding, and being present to a site *in whatever way works for you.* Feeling the subtle energies that are present in a place requires sensitivity and intuition. It is a bit like tuning a radio dial to a particular frequency. These techniques can be taught (we have studied with several teachers who have taught us how). Such instruction is outside the scope of this guidebook, although we do give a few suggestions for how you can be more attuned to a powerful place.

We encourage you to listen carefully to your own inner guidance as you open yourself to what may be available to you at a particular place on a particular day, at a particular time of day, with the particular predisposition you bring at that moment. You must use your own judgment about what is good or not good for you. Trust your feelings—and enjoy the mystery.

A few more things to notice

Ancient people often constructed several sites at some distance from each other. These sites often appear to have a visual (and probably energetic) relationship to each other and to prominent natural features such as hilltops, gaps between hills, etc. This phenomenon is called "intervisibility" and the landscapes themselves are called ritual landscapes. In other words, a powerful place should be experienced in relationship to its surroundings. Prominent ritual landscapes occur in the areas around the Calanais Stones in Scotland; the alignments at Carnac in Brittany; various sites in County Sligo, Ireland; the Nosterfield area in England; and Stonehenge in Wiltshire, England, among others. There is much speculation about the purpose of these landscapes, but it is increasingly clear that they exist and were created intentionally.

Not only were sacred sites constructed with an awareness of the energies of the earth and in relationship to each other and to surrounding natural features—they were also often built to interact with solar, lunar, or stellar events. For example, the light of the setting winter solstice sun shines into the entry passageway of Maeshowe, a site described in *Powerful Places in Scotland.* Just as churches used to be constructed so that the altar was in the east (facing the rising sun and signifying the resurrected Christ), so were many megalithic sites designed to take advantage of recurring seasonal astronomical events. Unfortunately, it is often difficult to prove which, or how many, events were being marked.

Organization

Each chapter begins with a brief account by Elyn of a visit to a particular powerful place. This is followed by information about the site along with suggestions, quotations in grey boxes, and related graphics. At the end of each chapter are directions on how to get there and, often, a brief space (Notes) for you to add your own observations. The guidebook concludes with a glossary and bibliography.

How did we choose these particular locations? We talked with people; we did research in books and on the web to discover possible powerful places that were not likely to be on every tourist's itinerary; we visited Brittany on several occasions with guides and without; and we paid attention to what we experienced at different sites. We then selected powerful places to include in this guidebook.

This specialized guidebook is not an exhaustive listing of all the powerful places in Brittany; to do that would require a much larger book. Nor is it a complete guide to what to see or where to stay in northwestern France. For that you'll need to consult a general travel book. This guidebook *is* intended as an invitation to experience powerful places in Brittany. We hope that it's the beginning of a conversation. We'd like to hear from you.

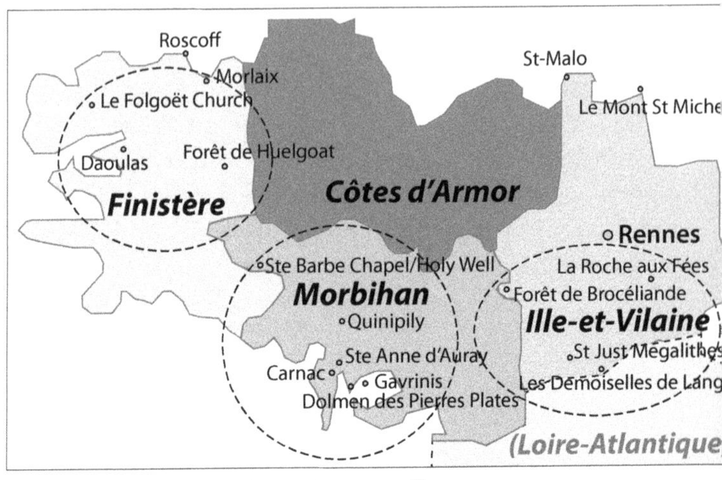

Exploring Brittany

The map above shows the three general areas included in this guidebook. When we have traveled in Brittany (Bretagne), we have based ourselves in the magic-filled Forêt de Brocéliande and in Carnac, near the standing stones, taking day trips to other sites. Next time, we might stay in Daoulas or Morlaix and spend more time near the northwest coast.

Water-lapped Brittany (with 1800 miles of deeply indented coastline) is the westernmost point of France. That's why one of its *départements* is called Finistère—the "End of the Earth." Brittany is composed of two distinct ecosystems: the coast, with its beautiful islands, sandy beaches, and rocky, windswept shores; and inland, which includes fertile fields, evocative forests, and ranges of hills (called mountains by the locals), moors, and heath. Although Brittany might seem isolated, it is a thriving economic hub of international importance. These activities range from maritime to agricultural to lace making to electronics—to tourism.

In many ways Brittany is diverse, but woven through the diversity is a strong, pervasive cultural identity: Breton. This identity traces itself back to the Celts, who arrived there more than 2500 years ago. The language (Breton, also called Brezhoneg, closely linked to Welsh and Gaelic), mythology, and music have strong Celtic roots. Each year, Lorient hosts the hugely popular Festival Interceltique, and many other Celtic music and cultural festivals occur throughout the year, including the popular *festou-noz,* nights of music, dancing, and entertainment.

There is something "different" about the Bretons, living in a land of mists and sea, of ancient woodlands and mysterious megaliths. Mystical and dreamy, they live at the edge of the world, perhaps in more ways than one....

Religion has played a vital part in Breton life throughout the millennia and religious observance is still quite strong. The local saints number in the hundreds, and deep devotion is widespread. Bretons still wear traditional costumes at the popular *pardons* (annual religious processions). The Tro Breizh or Tour of Brittany (www.brittanywalks.com/trobreizh.htm) is a 435-mile pilgrimage circuit that visits seven cathedrals in Brittany, where the faithful pay homage to the relics of Brittany's founding saints. Its heyday was in the fourteenth century, but loyal Bretons still walk the route. As you explore Brittany, you'll find numerous parish closes *(enclos paroissial)*, a religious complex consisting of a triumphal entrance, church, ossuary or charnel house, cemetery, and monumental calvary (a large crucifix, complete with biblical scenes). Some

> Sergio Berti, an Italian geobiophysical analyst, says Brittany has m
> places that affect the sympathetic component of the autonom
> nervous system. For example, an underground fault may reduce sy
> pathetic activity; granite may stimulate sympathetic activity; and r
> tallic minerals may stimulate activity or not, depending on the ty
> An increase in sympathetic activity is linked to action, optimism, a
> readiness to fight; A decrease is linked to relaxation, slower brea
> ing, and the predominance of the mind over body. (See p. 97.)

say the close resembles a giant passage grave. The dead are never far away in Brittany.

The earliest traces of human habitation in Brittany go back 500,000 years, to sites that are now beneath the sea, which rose dramatically 10,000 years ago at the end of the last glaciation. More numerous remains have been found dating back to 5000 BCE, when early inhabitants began to practice agriculture and herding. Little is known about the people who erected the numerous megaliths throughout the region. One of the oldest megalithic sites in Brittany (the huge Cairn de Barnenez) dates to 4600 BCE. This makes it much older than Stonehenge (2800 BCE) or the Great Pyramid (2550 BCE).

The Celts invaded Armorica ("Country near the Sea," as they called it) around 500 BCE, to be followed by the Romans in 56 BCE. Brittany ("Little Britain") gets its name from the numerous Welsh and Cornish Britons who settled there, beginning in the fifth century, fleeing Anglo-Saxon invaders. They brought with them British legends, hence the stories of Arthur, Merlin, Lancelot, and the Grail that continue to permeate the Breton atmosphere. They also brought Christian monks, bearing a Celtic strain of Christianity.

Over the centuries, other invaders tried to capture Brittany, and sometimes they succeeded. In the 800s, the Scandinavian Normans swept into the land, ransacking towns and monasteries. Throughout the centuries, Brittany struggled to maintain its independence from external powers—including France—and sometimes it succeeded, but it finally lost its independence to France in the early sixteenth century.

Although for centuries Brittany was a rural backwater, after World War II it made a remarkable recovery. No longer isolated, it is France's second most popular tourist destination and France's foremost producer of numerous farm products, as well as a center for high-tech industry. Throughout it all, the unique character of Brittany and the Bretons has endured.

Brittany is divided into four (or, according to the Bretons, five) major *départements*. Clockwise from the northeast, they are: Ille-et-Vilaine, Loire-Atlantique (part of Brittany until 1973 but now part of Pays de la Loire), Morbihan, Finistère, and Côte d'Armor. Each region has its own character, but we will not be focusing on regions. Instead, we will explore particular sites of unusual character: powerful places in Brittany.

Note: In French, Saint is abbreviated St and Sainte (feminine) is abbreviated Ste. Periods are not used after these abbreviations. Bretagne is pronounced "Bretanya," but the Bretons themselves refer to their country as Breizh. After years of repression, Breton and Gallo (a Romance language spoken in the eastern part of Brittany) are spoken by only a minority of Bretons. Also note: determining the age of a megalith is not an exact science. As a result, different sources may give different dates.

Sacred Brittany

Ah, Brittany. We have returned again and again to her sea-swept shores, drawn by her mysterious megaliths, her holy wells, her medieval villages, her pilgrimage churches, her magical forests and Merlin myths. The first time we visited the Forêt de Brocéliande, the remnants of the great primeval forest that once covered northwestern France, we realized we had entered into a "thin" place, a place where the veil between consensual reality and the realm of spirits is easily crossed. It isn't only in the forest, however, that one senses this interstitial shift. This interpenetration of one world with another can also occur at the standing stones, inside the tumuli with their intriguing carvings, or beside a sacred spring.

Admittedly, we have been enchanted by Brittany. Also admittedly, when we brought some friends there a few years ago, they were not. A few days of visiting our favorite sites was enough for them; they hopped on a train and escaped to Paris. There's no guarantee that Brittany will lure you in the way it has lured us, but we encourage you to be open to that possibility.

The following brief introduction will orient you to some of the different kinds of powerful places in Brittany.

Healing Springs

Our bodies are approximately 60% water: we need to drink water to stay alive. We also use water for cleansing, purification, and transformation. Water is a central part of baptismal rites around the world. It is also associated with healing: certain sources of water, flowing up from the ground or out of the side of a hill, have been thought to help cure various maladies. This water comes from the realm of the unseen, hidden in the earth, and brings some of that mysterious realm up into the light.

Some holy wells (natural springs with buildings over or walls surrounding them) are believed to heal eye problems, others address "female" issues, still others are purported to ameliorate skin diseases or nervous conditions. Holy wells are an opportunity to interact with the sacred.

> "Celtic sacred waters are associated with the three archetypes of light: the sun, the eye and consciousness. When we use sacred waters, we commune with these archetypes, which manifest themselves to us as deities, legends, traditions and folk practices." Nigel Pennick, *Celtic Sacred Landscapes*, p. 63.

Miraculous wells are very important in Brittany. At one time these wells may have had resident *anima loci* or were dedicated to particular deities. Now Christianized, many of these sacred springs are associated with saints or the Virgin Mary. People continue to visit them, seeking healing that they have not found through more conventional means.

Sacred Trees

Trees provide humans with fruits and nuts, with fuel, with wood for boats, shelter, furniture, weapons, and coffins. But trees are much more than objects for human use. Trees are vital to the wellbeing of the planet, helping to maintain the stability of the climate. They "inhale" carbon dioxide and release much-needed oxygen into the environment. They hold the soil in place and exchange nutrients with it. They provide home and haven for animals, insects, and birds.

At the symbolic level, a tree is an *axis mundi* (a cosmic axis) uniting the underworld, this world, and the heavens. Its roots are in the earth, its trunk in the air, and its branches reach toward the sky. Different trees have different mythic associations. Yggdrasil is the ancient ash tree that Norse mythology describes as an immense "world tree," complete with dragons entwining in its roots. Other examples of symbol-laden trees include the Trees of Life and Knowledge in the Garden of Eden, the Christmas evergreen, and the yule log.

According to Mara Freeman, in Celtic times "trees not only provided earthly sustenance: they were regarded as living, magical beings who bestowed blessings from the Otherworld. Wood from the nine sacred trees kindled the need-fire that brought back the sun to earth on May Eve; tree names formed the letters of the Ogham alphabet which made potent spells when carved on staves of yew; rowan protected the byre; ash lent power to the spear's flight." http://www.chalicecentre.net/celtic-treeoflife.htm

There is a difference between domesticated trees and an old-growth forest. Nigel Pennick asserts that "The wild wood is the place in which we can restore our conscious link with our inner instincts by contacting the 'wild man' within all of us. When we are supported by the elemental powers of the wood, a rediscovery of forgotten things can take place." *(Celtic Sacred Landscapes,* p. 24).

Trees were often linked with particular deities, but they were also thought to have their own resident spirits. Individual trees might be the source of great wisdom or inspiration. Living for hundreds of years, they became imbued with a kind of "personality." Greeks and Celts worshipped in sacred groves called *nemetoi* or *nemeton*. Certain forests were themselves considered sacred—including the Forêt de Brocéliande. Little remains of it now, except the Forêt de Huelgoat and the Forêt de Paimpont, where we will be spending some time.

They say that sometimes you can't see the forest for the trees—but sometimes you can't see the trees for the forest. It's easy to forget that each tree is unique, a living, breathing entity experiencing its life surrounded by its neighbors. In the Forêt de Brocéliande a number of very powerful, wise old beings manifest as trees. Beech and oak trees spread their heavy-laden branches wide and high. They have lived much longer than you and I and have much to tell and much to share. They speak a different language than words, and it takes a while to catch their meaning.

Sacred Stones

Stone: enduring, eternal—or at least closer to ageless than frail human flesh. Meditate on a stone and eons of geological time unfold before you. Perhaps that's part of the allure of the megaliths that we encounter throughout Brittany.

But that's not all. There's also the puzzle of what these sacred stones were used for. Perhaps it would be more accurate to say "stones used for sacred constructions," but we have felt on numerous occasions that the stones themselves were not just inert building blocks. They often seem to have their own energies, their own personalities. In Brittany we have visited numerous megalithic sites, dating from 5000-6000 years old or even older. We have pondered and puzzled over the significance of kilometer-long rows of standing stones, over the meaning of ornately carved slabs on the interior of earth-covered mounds; over the purpose of stone chambers, often called tombs but so much more than that.

A number of researchers have explored a variety of stone monuments, and they frequently report strange electro-magnetic phenomena. Dowsers often discover underground lines of energy or water threading beneath the stones; psychics may experience strange guardian-like figures or shadows of ancient rites. Whatever they were, whatever they remain, we find ourselves drawn to these megalithic sites, evocative and puzzling, revealing and hiding themselves with the changing of the day, the turning of the seasons.

> "Water-lines, blind springs and
> like aren't real, physical 'things' at
> they are ways of defining and descr
> ing the apparent lines and points
> the surface that coincide with cert
> kinds of definable water-flows bel
> You could call them a 'constructed
> ality,' an imaginary reality, in the sa
> way that the image on a radar scre
> or television screen is a reconstructi
> of reality." Tom Graves, *Needles of St*
> *Revisited*, p. 25.

Take your pick: standing stones that tower over your head, alignments that spread across the landscape in ordered rows and stretch on for miles, quadrilateral enclosures, stone circles, earth-covered cairns, table-like dolmens, their walls covered with mysterious carvings, huge horizontal slabs.... Find one that calls to you and draw near, breathing slowly, contemplating the slow breath of stone. See what you discover as the minerals in your bones and skin and hair respond to the minerals that make up these silent monoliths. Take your time. Slow down. They've been there for millennia. They don't divulge their secrets quickly—and never to a casual tourist.

Experiencing a Powerful Place

This is a guidebook about *experiencing* places—not just seeing them. You may have already developed your own way to visit a powerful place. If not, the following may be of use.

Much of the time we humans operate on "automatic," hardly registering where we are or what we feel. Visiting a powerful place is an opportunity to be intentional and alert. In order to fully experience a powerful place, it is important to be present. Be really aware of your surroundings and of changes in yourself in response to your surroundings. We suggest an acronym, **BLESSING**, to help remember how to prepare to enter a powerful place—whether it is a forest, a church, or a stone circle.

BLESSING stands for: **B**reathe slowly and regularly, paying attention to your breath moving in and out. If you have a breathing practice, now is the time to do it. **L**ook and **L**isten within: what are you sensing internally? How do you feel? **E**stablish yourself in your location, perhaps by orienting to the seven directions (east, south, west, north, above, below, and the center within—or, before you, behind you, to your right, to your left, above, below, and the center within). **S**ense your surroundings, opening up your five senses (and sixth sense) to what is around you. **S**tate your **IN**tention to respect this place, to experience what is present. **G**ive gratitude for this opportunity.

One of our mentors, Mara Freeman, suggests the acronym **ECOLOGY** for remembering how to approach a stone circle. It can, of course, be modified to apply to powerful places in general. "E" stands for **E**ntry, which means enter by first circling the site in a clockwise (sunwise) direction. "C" is for **C**entering yourself. This is often best accomplished by touching one of the stones. "O" stands for **O**ffering, which can be a bit of grain, milk, a strand of hair, saliva, etc., which shows that you come in good faith. The best offerings are biodegradable so they don't linger in the environment to build up over time. "L" is for **L**istening—listen to the sounds around you: birds, wind, wild creatures, and other sounds of nature. "O" stands for **O**pening up your inner and outer senses. "G" is for **G**ratitude to the place, the Earth, all of life, and Nature. "Y" is for **Y**ou: you should leave a place just as you found it. Take nothing and leave nothing. You can see the result of people not observing this injunction at many popular sacred sites: trees damaged by people taking pieces of their bark or carving on them; sites littered with paper wrappers and trash; melted wax dripped over ancient stones. Observe **ECOLOGY**: the Earth and future visitors will thank you.

Before entering a church, temple, or tumulus, place your hand lightly on the column or stone to the right of the entryway. Pause a moment to attune yourself (come into energetic harmony) with the place. Then step *over* (not on) the threshold.

Elyn Aviva

Tumulus St-Michel, Carnac, with chapel on top

Around Carnac

Nowhere in the known world has as many megalithic sites as Brittany, and Carnac is in the center of them. Human habitation in Carnac has been dated to 5700 BCE, probably making Carnac the longest continuously inhabited spot on earth. The amazing profusion of ancient remains includes standing stones, alignments that go on for kilometers, tumuli, quadrilaterals, stone enclosures, and dolmens, each with its own energy, its own story.

Much of the vocabulary used to describe megaliths (Greek for "big stones") is Breton. A single standing stone is a *menhir* (Breton for "long stone"); a table-like stone structure is a *dolmen*; a circle or enclosure of stones is a *cromlech*. A *cairn* is a pile of stones over a dolmen. In addition (though not of Breton origin) a tumulus is an artificial earth mound built over a stone chamber, often reached by a passageway; a quadrilateral is a rectangular arrangement of standing stones; and an alignment is a row of *menhirs*.

The area around Carnac also has numerous holy wells (natural springs with protective constructions around them), chapels and abbeys, beaches, thalassotherapy spas, delicious seafood, and butter-drenched Breton desserts. We will describe some of our favorite powerful places and point you in the direction of others. Take a walk in the forest, a ramble through the woods, and you'll discover your own.

Getting There

You can arrive in Brittany by air, train, or auto ferry from England. Regular airline and train services run

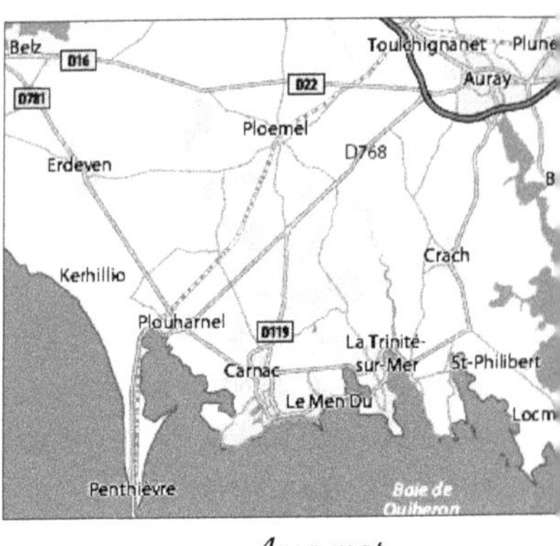

Area map

between Paris and Rennes. Depending on the season, you may be able to continue by train to Plouharnel, which is just northwest of Carnac (http://www.sncf.com/en_EN/flash/). Brittany Ferries offers regular service from Portsmouth, England, to St. Malo and from Plymouth, England, to Roscoff. There is also a ferry from Cork, Ireland, to Roscoff (http://www.brittanyferries.com/). Once you get to Brittany, you will probably want to rent a car to visit the numerous sites, many of which are in rural areas. A good map is essential, and a GPS will make your excursions easier.

To reach Carnac by car, take D768 southwest from Auray and exit on D119 toward Carnac. This highway crosses the alignments north of town; you can drive on the Route des Alignements or Route de Kerlescan, which passes just south of Le Ménec, Kermario, and Kerlescan alignments. The main visitors' center, Maison des Mégalithes, is on the Route des Alignements. From the Maison, you can ride Le Petit Train for a tour around the Carnac area (www.Petittrain-carnac.com). The tourist offices in town provide an excellent map showing numerous megalithic sites. Hiking trails link many of the megaliths.

Alignements de Carnac (Carnac Alignments)

We drove around a corner and encountered an astounding sight: row after row of standing stones, stretching out to the horizon. "Pull over!" I demanded. Barely waiting for the car to stop, I opened the door, jumped out, and ran over to the fence that separated the stones from me. I shook my head in disbelief, in awe. They were beyond my understanding. So many stones, all lined up and going—where? Why? They fit no category I knew: an enormous puzzle of countless granite megaliths pointing to the sky, rooted in the earth. Hundreds, thousands of stones lined up in slightly undulating rows that went on for several kilometers, as if the stones were frozen in the act of marching—somewhere. What was the point? What did they mean? What were they for? *The stones made no response. (Elyn)*

"Are there places in our landscape that act as gates to the past? Or, if not the past as such, parallel but subtly different worlds? There are experiences from visionaries that indicate that both possibilities exist, and that certain neolithic sites were actually built to take advantage of this." Alan Richardson, *Spirits of the Stones*, pp. 103-104.

The small seaside town of Carnac is the site of over 3000 standing stones that are arranged in more-or-less parallel rows stretching over two miles. It is the largest collection of standing stones in the known world. They were probably erected beginning about 6500 years ago, although the dates are somewhat uncertain. In the 1800s it was assumed that the standing stones were of Celtic origin, but, although the Celts no doubt made use of them, the megaliths are much older. Crafted out of native granite, the alignments were originally part of a single continuous construction, but stones have been removed and roads cut through; they are now divided into several sections with different names.

The most important are the alignments of Le Ménec, Kermario, and Kerlescan. The alignments of Le Ménec include 1099 stones in eleven rows, while the Kermario alignments have 1029 stones in ten rows. The smaller alignment at Kerlescan is composed of 555 stones in thirteen rows. The alignments of Le Ménec end with a cromlech, the remains of which forms part of the village of Le Ménec. The village is a good place to view the stones and also has a small *crêperie* that serves the local buckwheat *galettes*.

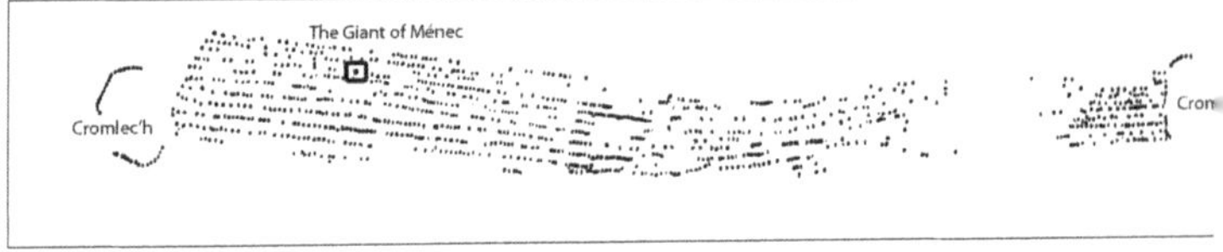

Alignements du Ménec

Although humans have lived with these puzzling rows of stones for millennia, there was little interest in studying them until the nineteenth century. In the 1860s James Miln, a Scottish antiquarian, did a thorough study and reported that fewer than 700 of the stones were still standing. Around 1875 he engaged a local boy, Zacharie Le Rouzic, to help him with his investigations. Le Rouzic devoted his life to the stones, re-erecting many of them and directing the James Miln Museum in Carnac (now called the Musée de Préhistoire), established to house many of

Gary pointing to Le Rouzic's red cement

the archaeological finds the two made over the years. Le Rouzic was careful in his work to clearly identify the stones that he raised, marking each with a small square of embedded red cement that remains visible today.

Although the exact original placement of individual stones is uncertain, there has been considerable speculation about the connection of the stones to astronomical events such as the rising or setting of the sun at the solstices. In 1970, Scottish engineer Alexander Thom produced a series of papers on the astronomical alignments of the stones and proposed a standard form of measurement, which he called the "megalithic yard." A different theory about the original purpose of the stones was proposed by Pierre Méreaux in 2001. Méreaux notes that the area around Carnac is the center of considerable seismic activity and that the stones may have been erected at delicate points to act as earthquake detectors. The idea that the stones may have been a form of

Elyn Aviva

Alignements du Ménec

"The focal points, the node points in th matrix of energies, are the equivalent acupuncture-points on a landscape sca And set into these points are 'needl not just of stone . . ." Tom Graves, *Need of Stone Revisited*, p. 68.

"earth acupuncture" is also widespread. The purpose would be to draw off energy from the earth faults (of which there are many) and help stabilize the land—as well as to unite earth and heaven.

The alignments have been fenced off by the Ministère de la Culture and direct access is restricted. In the 1990s, only guided tours were allowed. The rules have been relaxed in recent years, due in part to the activities of a local group that has engaged in civil disobedience of various sorts to protest government attempts to restrict access (http://www.menhirslibres.org/welcome.html). Some "sensitives" claim the stones have been losing energy since they have been fenced in. This raises interesting questions about the interaction between people and the stones.

Cartoon from the Menhirs Libres *website*

At present you have to view most of the alignments from outside the fences, but you may be allowed inside one section or another on a guided tour, depending on the

Alignements du Ménec

time of year and the whims of government officials. However, there is a site (see p. 33) where another set of alignments is unfenced and open to the public.

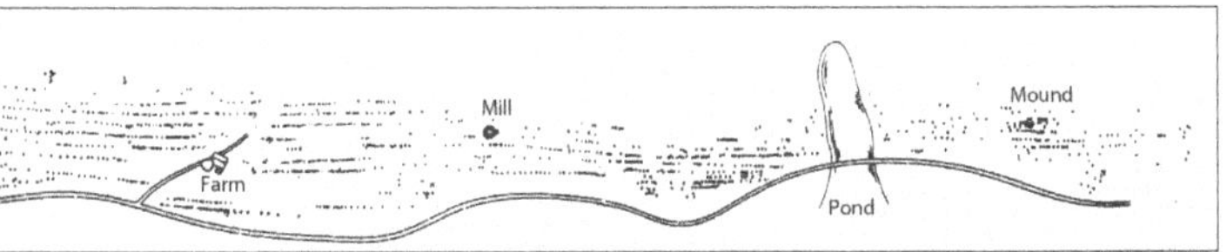

Alignements de Kermario

Entry into the Carnac alignments requires a ticket, available at the Maison des Mégalithes across from Le Ménec. Here you can purchase maps, guides, and tickets. Be sure to get a "Pass des Mégalithes," which you can use at the Musée de Préhistoire de Carnac, Cairn de Gavrinis, Cairn du Petit Mont à Arzon, Carnac Alignements, and Site des Mégalithes de Locmariaquer. We visit Gavrinis and Locmariaquer later in this guidebook (see pp. 53-65). You pay full-price for the first site you visit and get a discount on the others.

While the Carnac alignments are the central megalithic attraction for tourists, we encourage you to explore farther afield. Standing stones, alignments, dolmens, and tumuli abound in the area. Many are well marked with signs along the roads, but others are known only to locals. We will be discussing some of these megalithic sites in subsequent sections. (http://www.france-for-visitors.com/brittany/index.html, http://www.ot-carnac.fr/ and www.carnac.monuments-nationaux.fr)

Elyn Aviva

Géant du Manio

Quadrilatère and Géant du Manio (The Quadrilateral and Giant of Manio)

I'd been there before but never really "got" it. I'd seen a bunch of stones arranged in a large trapezoid (the Quadrilateral) with a 21-foot-high megalith (the Giant) in a nearby clearing. This time, however, I had read a research paper analyzing the site, so I looked in the woods for the recumbent "La Dame du Manio" stone and a square stone that lined up with it. I found them, but I was not convinced. I thought: it's just a bunch of chance associations. "Seeing" wasn't enough. I had to experience something.

Dowsing rods, compass, and suddenly a grand "aha!" There was nothing random about the placement of these stones, I realized. The giant stone casts its shadow through a slit in the Quadrilateral wall; the domed La Dame establishes the geometry. I stood in the middle of the triangle formed by La Dame, the Square Stone, and the Géant—and I felt a powerful buzz. Suddenly I understood. I was standing in a carefully designed, meticulously engineered, megalithic ceremonial site, based on the pregnant swelling of La Dame, rising out of Mother Earth. (Elyn)

Coming to Le Quadrilatère and Géant du Manio after a walk through the woods is impressive. The standing stone called the Géant is one of the tallest standing stones in Europe. The approximately 120-foot by 30-foot Quadrilatère is neatly laid out with stones that are more-or-less equal in size—except for two. More about those later.

We had visited this site several times in the past and marveled at the ancient architects' work. However, this time we had a copy of Robin Heath's article

Quadrilatère

"The Discovery of a Soli-lunar Calendar Device Within an Astronomical Ritual Complex at Le Manio, Morbihan, Brittany." We planned to check out his equinox and solstice alignment theories (see drawing below). We were doubtful that we would find anything that would convince us of the validity of his rather complicated set of angles and triangles. Two of his important marking stones (La Dame and the Pierre Carrée) are found in the woods outside the low stone walls that mark the modern limits of the site.

Gary stood at the Géant and began dowsing. He found a prominent underground fault line that leads from the stone toward the Quadrilatère. When he checked out the direction of this line he saw that it headed straight for the vulva-shaped opening between two taller stones in the Quadrilatère. (The fault line is not absolutely straight, but the general direction is clear.) These two stones are the

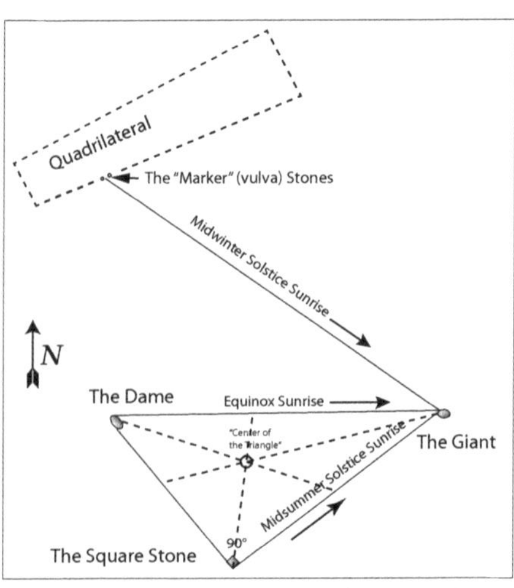

Drawing of the Manio site (adapted from Robin Heath's article)

marker stones that Heath identifies as being in alignment with the midwinter solstice sunrise. If you stand behind those two stones at winter solstice and sight through the opening toward the Géant, you will see the sun rise directly behind the Géant. Of course, it's always possible that because the Géant has been re-erected, this astronomical alignment is just an artifact—but Gary's dowsing seems to affirm Heath's theory.

Elyn Aviva

The "marker" (vulva) stones

Next we climbed over the modern stone walls and searched the woods for two stones that are known as La Dame du Manio (the Lady or Queen of Manio) and the Pierre Carrée (the Square Stone). They were easily found, in part because the underbrush has been cleared around them. La Dame is a dome-shaped rock that projects about eighteen inches above ground level. It appears to be the top of a much larger stone that is mostly buried. Gary thinks it is the original bedrock of the area. The Pierre Carrée is easily identified since it is nearly square and about eighteen inches high. La Dame is directly west of the Géant; the Pierre Carrée forms a 90° angle with lines

La Dame du Manio

Pierre Carrée (Square Stone)

from La Dame and the Géant. We did not confirm these observations with surveying tools, but Heath did.

We were not at the site at the equinoxes or the solstices, so we couldn't confirm Heath's other two conclusions about this triangle, nor did we attempt to validate his lunar calendrical observations. Nevertheless, we left convinced that this stone complex was an ancient ceremonial center and an astronomical observatory. Presumably those functions were inseparable.

On a subsequent visit to the site with our friend and dowsing instructor Anne Parker, we were able to confirm our previous observations and dowsing conclusions. Anne suggested that the focal point of the right triangle formed by the Géant, La Dame, and the Pierre Carrée might be a highly energetic spot (see drawing, p. 28). We each took a turn standing on that point; the energy was indeed pal-

"From the evidence discovered by Crowhurst and the ACEM [Association pour la Connaissance les Etudes des Megalithes] team, the Le Manio site is clearly built to indicate the key times of the solar year, solstices, and equinoxes, within a ritually significant monument that presents the cycle of the year within an analogue of human life—conception to birth and, one might surmise, rebirth." Robin Heath, "The Discovery of a Soli-lunar Calendar Device Within an Astronomial Ritual Complex at le Manio, Morbihan, Brittany," p. 7. http://www.skyandlandscape.com/pdf/LeManio.pdf.

The sign pointing to the site

pable. Anne believes the site is a magnificently conceived teaching center for megalithic master builders.

Gary feels that La Dame is the key to the site. Assuming it is, indeed, bedrock, the other stones would have been erected based on its (immovable) location. One wonders why this stone is called "La Dame": because it resembles a pregnant belly rising out of the earth? Or because it is the true center—"the Queen"—of the site?

We encourage you to visit this site. If you find La Dame, the Square Stone, and the center of the triangle, you may experience more than the casual tourists who simply look at the site, have a picnic on the stone walls, and walk on. The stones are impressive (look for the Géant's face in the photo on p. 26).

Getting There

To go to the Quadrilatère and Géant du Manio drive (or walk) on the Route de Kerlescan past the Alignements de Kermario until you come to the equestrian center. Park just before the center and follow the well-marked trail, turning left at the sign (see photo above).

Notes

Elyn Aviva

One of the Géants de Kerzerho

Alignements de Kerzerho near Erdeven

A road slices through the stone alignments, but it doesn't matter. Leave your car in the parking lot and walk among the massive megaliths, stroll between the rows. Traffic noise fades away. Deep peace prevails. Come at sunrise, noon-rise, and sunset, experience the shifting energies of the stones as they awake from slumber, gather energy, and sink into quiet with the turning of the day. Walking between the rows, I feel my cells align, like iron filings drawn into pattern by a magnet. A bird chirps; the trees are in bloom. I walk farther, coming to the remains of an important ceremonial site: giant standing stones, several huge menhirs lying prone. I feel called to lean back against a standing stone and meditate. (Elyn)

Although the alignments of Carnac have become a tourist attraction that can be seen but rarely touched—viewed but not "encountered"—an impressive set of alignments just five and one half miles away is not fenced in. Leave Carnac going northwest toward Erdeven on D781. Just before the city limits the Kerzerho Alignments line both sides of the road. What you see are the remains of ten rows of stones that may have extended for over a mile 5000 years ago. Many stones have been removed over the centuries, but this is still a very powerful place. Long ago, a road was cut through the alignments and

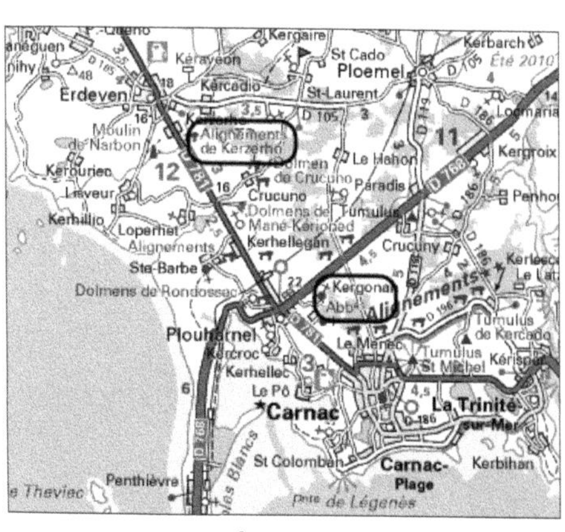

Area map

Alignements de Kerzerho

houses were built among the stones. While this defaced this ancient site, it may have protected it from later government interference.

You can leave your car in the parking lot and walk directly into the alignments. Take time to center yourself. Use one of the techniques we suggest on p. 16 or any centering technique that you have learned. Walk slowly among the stones and note any subtle changes that you feel. Within the alignments the atmosphere is somehow different from that on the "outside."

We have walked among these alignments many times over the years and have come to appreciate these granite stones as old friends. It was while walking in these alignments several years ago that Gary had the strong intuition that at least part of the energetic effects that he felt was due to being in the middle of so much granite. We know that granite has considerable piezoelectric (production of electrical current in response to mechanical strain) properties. Our bones also

Elyn Aviva

Another view

> Looking at people's experiences so far, it does seem that these sacred places, these mysterious stones and mounds and circles, were built to do something. It does seem they were expressions of a kind of magickal technology that relied upon something within the mind of the individual to make it work. Something that mankind has, over the millennia, lost touch with, and that is intimately connected with time and other-dimensional awareness." Alan Richardson, *Spirits of the Stones*, pp. 122.

possess similar piezoelectric properties. Perhaps when we walk through a field of granite stones, they induce subtle electrical fields within our bodies. If this is true, there may be sensations generated while walking that are discharged by contact with the stones themselves. Whatever the mechanism, we feel a sense of inner "alignment" amongst the stones.

It is documented that Roman and, later, Breton farmers drove their cattle through the alignments, apparently believing this was beneficial for the animals. This "healing effect" has been proposed as an original purpose for the stones, but that is pure speculation. The annual "*pardon* of the horned beasts" at the church of St. Cornély in Carnac (see p. 39) is a Christianization of this ancient ritual.

Les Géants de Kerzerho

There is much more to experience at Kerzerho. Near the parking area and to the left of the alignments you will see a small

Elyn Aviva

The sign to the Géants

Géants de Kerzerho

sign (nearly obliterated) pointing to "Les Géants de Kerzerho." Follow the trail to a group of very large granite menhirs. Most are lying down, but a few are still upright. Spend as long as you can, sensing the energies of the different stones. It is not known if all of these stones were originally standing.

The large recumbent stone at the end of this group is known locally as the "Table du Sacrifice." This evocative name probably originated when standing stones were thought to be Celtic Druid ceremonial sites. Now we know they were erected thousands of years before the Celts arrived.

We have visited the alignments at Kerzerho at different times of the day, and we sense a shift in energy in the stones associated with the daily cycle of the sun. When we arrived before dawn the energy was very subdued and we had a feeling that the stones "awakened" with the rising sun. One might speculate that the effect of the sun striking the stones generated internal strain due to expansion caused by the sun's heat and we were somehow sensing that shift.

Another view

Take some time to walk among these ancient stones and see what you experience. Perhaps you will feel attracted to one or another. Do you sense differences in their "personalities"? If you return at sunset or high noon, do you sense a difference in the alignments?

More to Experience

If you are at Kerzerho Alignments in the afternoon, we highly recommend a visit to the Benedictine Abbaye Sainte-Anne-de-Kergonan for the vespers service (see map on p. 33). (http://www.plouharnel.fr/gb/decouvrir/patrimoine.html) In Plouharnel, take D768 in the direction to Auray. Watch for signs. (The nuns in the nearby Abbaye Ste-Michel-de-Kergonan also chant.)

Sunday vespers in the church; afternoon light shining through the windows. Simplicity brings inner quiet; my breath slows down, becomes deep and rhythmic. The monks process into the nave, greeting and bowing to each other, their black robes swinging rhythmically. The incense censor swings rhythmically, and fragrant smoke billows to the four directions. Everything is formal, carefully choreographed. The monks' clear voices rise in Gregorian chant, call and response, and in recitation. I think: if the standing stones could sing, is this what they would sound like? (Elyn)

North porch of Église St-Cornély

Église St-Cornély (St. Cornelius Church), Carnac

It's a friendly sort of church, nothing grandiose, not very old by French standards—built in the seventeenth century to honor Saint Cornelius, the patron saint of horned animals. When I learned this, my ears pricked up. Did I hear a faint echo of the antlered Celtic god Cernunnos—now morphed into a saint whose name is similar to the Latin word for "horn" (cornu)? *The coincidence made me wonder. Once upon a time, Roman and Breton herdsmen drove their cattle through the Carnac alignments to heal the animals of whatever ailed them; later, they took them to the church for Cornély's blessing. But why those stones? And why this church? And why Cornély? (Elyn)*

At first glance, Carnac's seventeenth-century church, dedicated to St Cornély, would seem to have little relationship to the nearby standing stones. But scratch beneath the surface and you'll find a number of connections. Christian missionaries arrived in Brittany in the fifth and sixth centuries to convert the pagan population. They assimilated local customs and beliefs and overlaid them with a Christian veneer.

The native people of Brittany—including the megalith builders—were farmers and herders. The megalith builders had domesticated animals, including sheep and cattle, and there is evidence of a Neolithic animal cult. Archeologists have discovered stag antlers and cattle horns buried inside some of the nearby dolmens, and horned animals and schematic horns are carved in stone inside some of the dolmens (for example at Gavrinis, p. 60). The Celts, millennia later, were also herders and farmers, and one of the gods in

Église St-Cornély

the Celtic pantheon was the horned god Cernunnos, the "Lord of the Stags." Finally, archeological evidence suggests that the Romans had a cattle cult and brought diseased animals to Carnac to be cured. Although the continuity of a bovine cult from Neolithic times can't be proved, the evidence is intriguing.

Conveniently for the efforts of the Christian missionaries, there was a legend (probably brought by the missionaries themselves) that a third-century pope called Cornelius just happened to have gone to Carnac. In 251 he was exiled from Rome, in part because he opposed the sacrificing of animals. Legend tells that at the outskirts of Carnac, he miraculously turned the Roman soldiers who were chasing him into stones: they became the alignments of Carnac.

Reliquary of St Cornély

Major offerings include money, grain r cattle. This offering is collected at a ecial ceremony held on the morning f September 13, the day of the fair of aint Cornély. The animals are brought the mill. Before the Mass, they are erded to the main entrance of the hurch, and the clergy comes out in rand style, with cross and banner, and lesses the herd, which consists mostly f cows, heifers and calves (sometimes orses and pigs). After the blessing, the attle are led before members of the estry at the fairgrounds where they re sold at auction." Description by acharie Le Rouzic (1909)

It seems likely that St Cornély was the Christian substitute for Cernunnos or his Roman replacement. A reliquary supposedly containing St Cornély's head can be seen in the church. Since the Celts had a cult of the head (important severed heads were consulted for advice, etc.), perhaps this was yet another way to draw upon local customs and shift them to Christian practices.

The residents of the region were known to drive their herds through the alignments to ensure their good health and well being. The Church assimilated (or co-opted, depending on your point of view) this practice. Until the 1950s, animals participated in the annual *pardon* and were blessed at St Cornély's holy fountain. When these cattle were sold at market they brought a premium price because people believed that they would protect their whole herd. Each year on the second Sunday of September there is a solemn mass followed by a procession, which is led by people carrying the reliquary of St Cornély.

Centuries ago, this annual *pardon* had become so popular that the existing church could not contain the multitude. A larger one was needed. Work began in

St Cornély on west façade

1639, ending twenty years later with a Renaissance-style church and what is now the central nave of St-Cornély. The northern and southern naves were added later, as were other chapels. In 1792 the elaborate porch was added on the north of the building to compete the structure. On the west exterior wall of the church is a statue of St Cornély with a white and red ox on either side. This commemorates the legend that the saint came to Carnac with two oxen and hid in one of the oxen's ears (it *is* a legend, after all) while turning the Roman soldiers into stone.

The primary entrance to the church is through the north porch, which is covered with a canopy topped with an elaborate stone crown (see photo, p. 38). Local legend claims it is constructed out of menhirs.

Inside the Church

The interior is rather dark and cavelike. The atmosphere of the interior of the church is peaceful and quiet, and the church is clearly well-loved by the community. Laminated information sheets in several languages, including

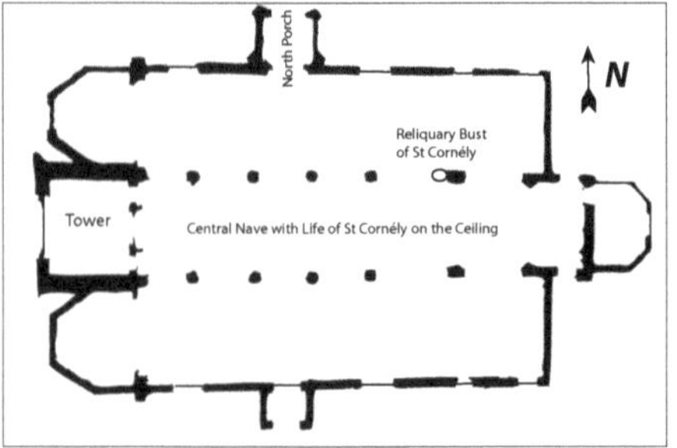

Plan of the church

English, are provided. There are several features worth noting. One is the reliquary bust of St Cornély, which is said to contain the saint's head—although a German monastery also claims to have that part of the saint's anatomy. The vault of the central nave contains charming eighteenth-century paintings depicting the life of St Cornély, as told in *The Golden Legend,* a popular retelling of saints' lives by Jacques de Voragine, a thirteenth-century Italian monk. It is worth spending time here and pondering the relationship between the animal cult, the alignments, St Cornély, and the church. Does "dark and cavelike" remind you of the inside of a covered dolmen? Maybe so.....

More to Experience

Carnac (population about 4500) is actually two small towns, Carnac-Ville and Carnac-Plage (Carnac Town and Carnac Beach). We have based ourselves in Carnac-Ville, which is closer to the megaliths. It has a number of interesting *crêperies,* pastry shops, and the impressive Musée de Préhistoire. The Museum of Prehistory contains over 500,000 archaeological artifacts (6000 of which are on display) from the

Exhibit in the Museum of Prehistory

Tumulus St-Michel

Paleolithic through the Gallo-Roman period, but concentrates on the Neolithic (5500-2200 BCE), the period during which the megaliths were built. It is an excellent museum, with a number of displays of intriguing, engraved stone slabs from nearby dolmens. The museum is within easy walking distance from St Cornély church.

Constructed about 4500 BCE, the Tumulus St-Michel is an imposing man-made hill in the northeastern part of Carnac. It is 40 feet high, 410 feet long, and 197 feet wide and covers an extensive passage tomb. Although called a passage grave, it is probable this tumulus was much more than a burial site. On top of the tumulus is a chapel dedicated to St. Michael. It dates from the early nineteenth century and replaced the original chapel built in 1664. [Note: you will often find chapels dedicated to St. Michael built on top of megalithic and pagan sites. The archangel is usually portrayed spearing a serpent or dragon—perhaps indicating that he has conquered the pagan religion or that he has control of the earth energies of the site.]

Elyn Aviva

Visiting La Fontaine St-Michel

While the underground passage

tomb has been closed every time we have visited, the tumulus itself is impressive. It was constructed about 6500 years ago without power equipment to move the stones and the earth. Near the tumulus is the holy well of St Michel; it can be reached by a foot path. Look for signs at the tumulus. The tumulus can be reached on foot from the downtown area, or you can drive and park at the nearby Hotel Tumulus.

Carnac has a number of holy wells or fountains, which are worth visiting. Compare what you feel at different wells. A good source of information is the *Guide pratique,* available from the excellent tourist information offices near the church and in Carnac-Plage (www.ot-carnac.fr).

South of Carnac (Carnac-Ville) is Carnac-Plage, a beachside resort town with six popular beaches. Carnac-Plage is also the home of the Carnac Thalasso & Spa Resort, a seawater spa.

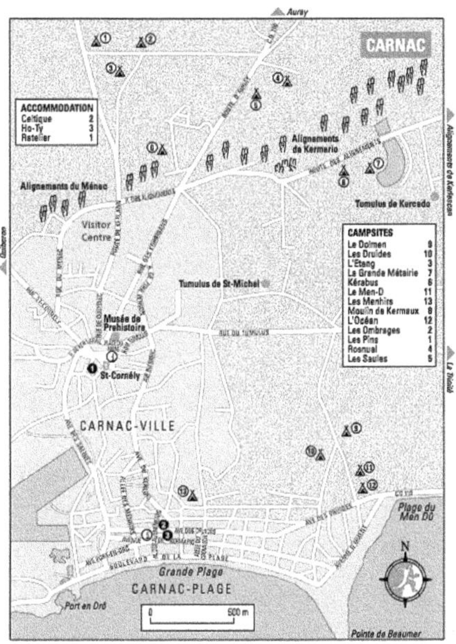

Elyn Aviva

Mané Bihan

Mané Bihan and Mané Braz

Our friendly Breton host offered to show us two of his favorite sites. "I go there when I'm sad, and then I feel better," Jean-François explained. He knew these primeval stones, grew up with them, visiting them the way you or I might go downtown to the drugstore or the movie theater—or to church.

He led us through the woods, losing the trail once or twice ("It must have been the korrigans*—the faeries," he explained, only half in jest). We arrived abruptly: a huge ring of stone, half-buried in the ground, covered with lichen. It was like an immense circular arcade—or had been, once. Now many of the rooftop stones were gone, the once-covered chambers open to the sky. This was no well-trampled site, its energies sucked out by casual tourists and irreverent visitors. No, this was the real thing. An ancient ring of stone hidden in the forest. A healing place. I wiped tears from my eyes. Our host smiled at my response and nodded. He knew, he knew. (Elyn)*

Don't try to find these megalithic sites on the web. You might or you might not find the ones we visited. Names are confusing, spellings differ, and descriptions vary. Suffice it to say that our knowledgeable Breton host, Jean-François, offered to show us two of his favorite megaliths, hidden in the woods. How could we say no? It was a rare opportunity to experience these ancient stones,

Elyn Aviva

Another view of Mané Bihan

Elyn Aviva

On the trail to the megaliths

far from the "madding crowds" of tourists.

We followed D16 from Locoal-Mendon (northwest of Auray) in the direction of Belz. Just before the Church of Ste Marguerite and the hamlet of Hent Gwenn, we parked the car at a dirt pull-off to the left of the main road. If you reach Kergleven you've gone too far.

Jean-François explained that Hent Gwenn means "White Way." Why "White Way"? Because the route once led to the alignments at Carnac and Erdeven. Why "white"? He said something that we understood to equate "white" with "sacred." (We communicated in a mixture of French, Breton, Spanish, and English, so something may have gotten lost in translation.)

Leaving the car, we crossed over a wooden barrier and into the woods. We followed Jean-François up a wide, well-marked path that even included botanical signposts. We left the trail and walked through the woods, soon arriving at Mané Bihan (Little Mountain).

It was awesome. It appears to be a partially covered cromlech or perhaps a huge, ring-like dol-

Detailed view of Mané Bihan

> we find ourselves engaged by a sa-ed place, and have our conscious-ss provoked by it, the reason such cations seem sacred, seem to pos-s a *numen loci,* may be precisely that receive more information from em. The very fact that there are, d have always been, sacred places monstrates their psychological im-rtance. They may be where we get greater glimpse of reality." Paul De-reux, *Re-Visioning the Earth,* p. 102.

men. We'd never seen anything like it, and Jean-François said it's the only one he knows. Originally the ring of stones had been entirely covered, but now many of the capstones and some of the chambers are missing. It is evocative, alluring, mysterious—and very moving. Center yourself and experience the "atmosphere" around the stones.

If you find Mané Bihan, spend a lot of time there. Be sure to stand in the center of the space enclosed by the stone ring and sense the energy. It's quite special.

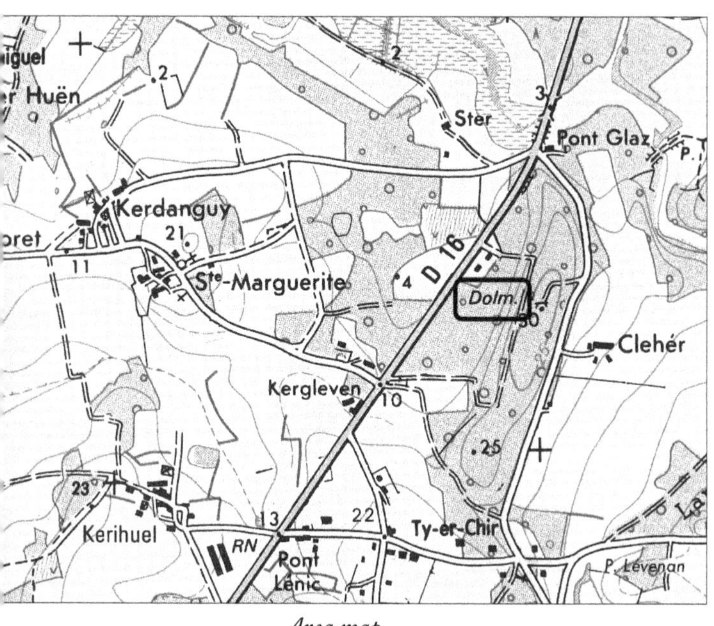

Area map

Mané Braz

From there we followed a wide trail in the beechwood forest, then climbed some steps up an embankment. Mané Braz (Big Mountain) is a large, curving dolmen on top of the "hill" called Mané Loc'h. Someone had held a ceremony there; a huge pine cone rested in the center of a circle of small stones inside one of the covered chambers. There were other megaliths nearby, perhaps the remains of other dolmens. This, too, is a very special place—and quite different in "feel" from Mané Bihan.

Imagine yourself growing up surrounded by these stones in the forest. Imagine walking as a child, discovering a moss-covered megalith.... Elyn asked Jean-François what it was like, growing up with the alignments, the dolmens, as his neighbors. He said something like, "We don't know what they were built for, but they're our heritage and we respect

Elyn Aviva

Inside Mané Braz

Another view of Mané Braz

them. They were built before the Celts, but the Celts respected them. And you feel good around them. Peaceful, calm."

We asked Jean-François if we should keep these places secret. At first he said "yes," but then he changed his mind. "It's all right to tell people. It's good for Brittany, and especially Locoal-Mendon, if some interested people know and respect this area. Anyway, this place will be public soon."

If you have the good fortune to have Jean-François take you on a visit, or if you befriend a local Breton who is willing to show you his or her favorite megaliths—treat them with all the honor and respect they are due. You are being given a very special gift.

More Information

Jean-François le Quéré and his wife, Nicole, own several lovely *gîtes* (vacation rentals). We stayed at Bod-Keriz (The Wild Cherry Orchard). There is some information about nearby sites on their website, http://www.pennti-mammig.com. Click on Bod-Keriz, then click on "location."

There are many megaliths off the beaten tourist track. It is worth finding them. To do so, you'll need either a helpful guide or a detailed topo map (for example IGN 0821 OT, "TOP 25") or both.

Elyn Aviva

Interior of Dolmen des Pierres-Plates

Mégalithes, Locmariaquer

We walk past the caravan park, stumble over the sand dunes, looking for the half-buried dolmen. A standing stone stands tall like a sentinel. "This way," it beckons. We see it, its entrance like a wide-gaping mouth, sticking out of the sand. Watching our heads (it was low in front) we slowly creep our way down the entry corridor, flashlight glinting on the stones. Engravings spring into light, then fade back. What were they there *for? And what were* we *there for? Mysteries abound. (Elyn)*

The Locmariaquer area is rich with megalithic sites. Most people visit the Site des Mégalithes, located at the entrance to the town. The ensemble includes an information center and three impressive megaliths. First, the 66-foot-long, 300-ton Grand Menhir Brisé, which lies in four pieces where it accidentally fell or was deliberately toppled. It is made of a kind of granite found 7.5 miles away and was somehow hauled to its current location. It has an axe carved on one side.

Elyn Aviva

Grand Menhir Brisé

Next, the 6000-year-old Table des Marchand, a reconstructed dolmen with a 23-foot-long corridor leading to a "funerary chamber." (We're not convinced that dolmens were burial chambers—even if human remains are found inside. That's like calling

Interior of Table des Marchand

Westminster Cathedral a cemetery!) The spacious "funerary chamber" has a large stele carved with crooks. Pieces of the engraved menhir that forms the ceiling are found in a nearby dolmen and at Gavrinis (see p. 60), raising intriguing questions about the ancient re-use of megalithic stones. Were the carvings no longer important and the stone conveniently available for re-use? Or did the carvings carry with them a certain kind of empowerment or sacredness, so it didn't matter if the stone was broken and re-used? As of now, nobody knows. The ceiling slab at Table des Marchand is engraved with axe and crook motifs and—remember Cernunnos, the cattle, and St Cornély?—the lower part of a bovine figure.

The third megalith is the immense Er-Grah Tumulus, long forgotten but rediscovered in 1991. It cannot be entered today. Archeologists believe it was originally a "closed-grave burial."

Although the displays in the information center are interesting, the Site des Mégalithes is effectively a theme park; it has turned the megaliths into objects

Sign for Dolmen des Pierres-Plates

to be seen, not experienced. We suggest that instead of spending much time at the site, pick up a detailed map at the Tourist Office in Locmariaquer (or buy IGN 0921 OT TOP 25 and IGN 0821 OT TOP 25 topo maps) and explore the area. Don't forget to bring a flashlight.

You'll find a number of fascinating megalithic sites, including two of the oldest dolmens in the area, the Dolmen de Mané-Lud (near the Site des Mégalithes, it has carved interior stones) and the Dolmen de Mané-Rethual (it also has carved interior stones). The enormous Tumulus de Mané-Er-Hroech (reached by a stairway with 23 steps) is also worth a visit, although the rich furnishings of axes and pendants of precious stones are now on display in the Vannes' Musée d'Histoire et Archéologie.

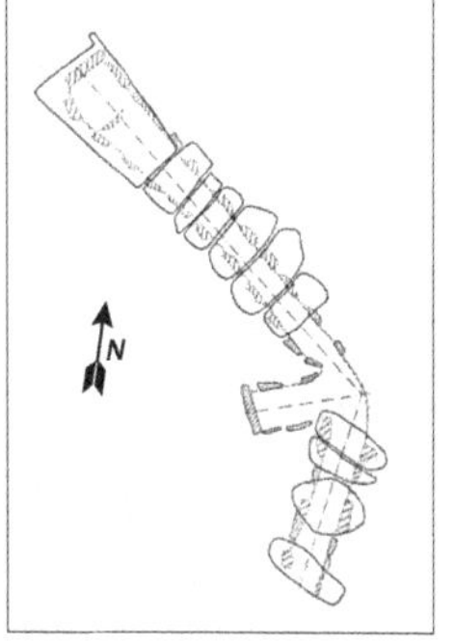

Plan of Pierres-Plates

Dolmen des Pierres-Plates

One of our favorite megalithic sites is the 5000-year-old Dolmen des Pierres-Plates, a short drive south and then west from Locmariaquer. There are bigger and older dolmens in Brittany, but Pierres-Plates has three important qualities. It is open to the public without a guide, which means you can spend as much time as you want inside, and it has fascinating engravings on the interior supporting stones. Its isolated location also means it isn't swarming with tourists—unless you go on a busy summer day.

Interior of Pierres-Plates

Although it is currently located in the middle of sand dunes, the sea level was lower when it was built. Pierres-Plates (meaning "flat stones") is 79 feet long. It has two chambers, linked by a long corridor that comes in at an angle. The entry corridor is 20 feet long; after it reaches a small chamber on the left (west) it turns at a 120° angle and continues to a large rear chamber.

Beginning at the entrance, a number of the interior upright stones have carvings on them. You can see them with a well-directed flashlight beam. Some of the carvings appear to be schematic represen-

Elyn Aviva

Engraved stone in Pierres-Plates

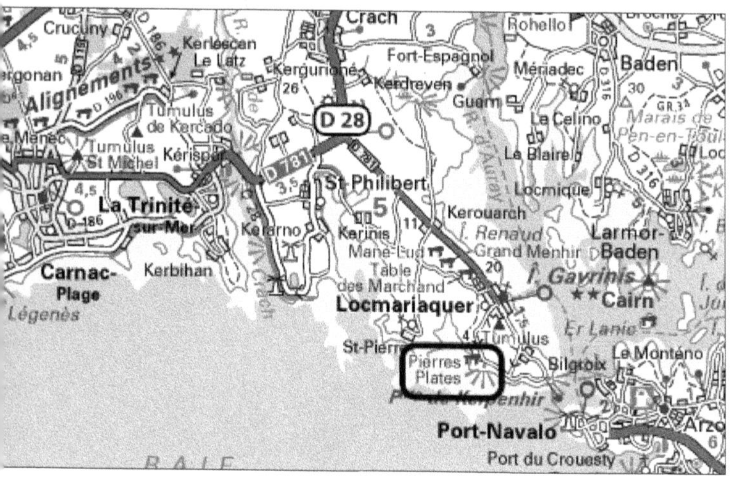

Area map

tations of the ancient Mother Goddess. Spend time alone in the (relative) darkness, if you can. Center yourself and see what you experience.

Getting There

Locmariaquer is a pleasant coastal town on the Gulf of Morbihan. It is near Carnac and only ten kilometers (six miles) east of La Trinité-sur-Mer via D781. The Site des Mégalithes is at the entrance to the town, near the cemetery. It is well signposted. Don't forget, the discount "Pass des Mégalithes" includes the "Site des Mégalithes de Locmariaquer." The Dolmen des Pierres-Plates is located south and west of Locmariaquer, just a bit inland from the Plage (Beach) de Locmariaquer. It is well signposted. You'll need to park in the nearby parking lot and walk a short distance toward the beach to find the path.

Plan to spend a day driving and walking around the peninsula visiting different megalithic sites, enjoying the beaches, and eating really fresh seafood.

Elyn Aviva

Interior of Gavrinis Cairn

Cairn de Gavrinis, Golfe du Morbihan

We arrive by boat and slowly climb the hill to the sacred mound. Eagerly, I enter into the darkness of the lengthy corridor. My eyes adjust. The upright slabs that line this stony birth canal are engraved with mysterious whorls, concentric arcs, axes, undulations, shields, and hooks. Energy patterns cut in stone? Marks of the Goddess, her priestesses, the local clans? The corridor widens and we stand close together in a womb-like chamber. Are we about to be reborn? Or have we already entered the Otherworld? Outside, the sun still burnishes the land, the waves still suck greedily at the shore. Inside, all is still. I hold my breath, waiting. I should not have come here without permission, without an offering. (Elyn)

Gavrinis Cairn is an amazing megalithic monument, built approximately 3500 BCE, though it might be older. We've visited Gavrinis three times, and each time has been too brief. Each time, we discover anew its enigmatic beauty.

From the outside, Gavrinis Cairn is imposing. It is located on a hillside on the southern end of Gavrinis Island, overlooking the Golfe du Morbihan and with a view of the River Auray. Almost 20 feet high and 164 feet in diameter, the earthen mound (tumulus) covers a stone cairn, which covers a so-called "passage grave," although it does not appear that anyone was buried there. It was built 500 years before Newgrange in Ireland and 800 years before the Great Pyramids of Egypt.

The dolmen is 52 feet in length, making it one of the longest dolmens in France; its straight passageway

Entrance to Gavrinis Cairn

is 46 feet long. [NB: measurements are approximate.] This corridor leads to a nearly square chamber, just over eight feet on each side. The chamber (some say it was a royal tomb, but we doubt that—especially since no burials have been found) is located almost exactly in the center of the cairn. The chamber's capstone is made of a single granite slab. During reconstruction work, archeologists discovered that this ceiling stone was originally part of a carved menhir from Locmariaquer, another piece of which is found in the ceiling of Table des Marchand (see p. 53). The capstone at Gavrinis was oriented with the carving (part of a bovine) uppermost, thus hiding it from view until the restoration work was undertaken. Was the carving no longer important, or was it not important that it be visible?

The stone-fronted façade, reconstructed in 1981 to resemble a step pyramid, is oriented to the rising sun at mid-winter solstice (as are Newgrange and La Roche aux Fées, among other megalithic monuments). For a few days, the sunlight pierces the corridor

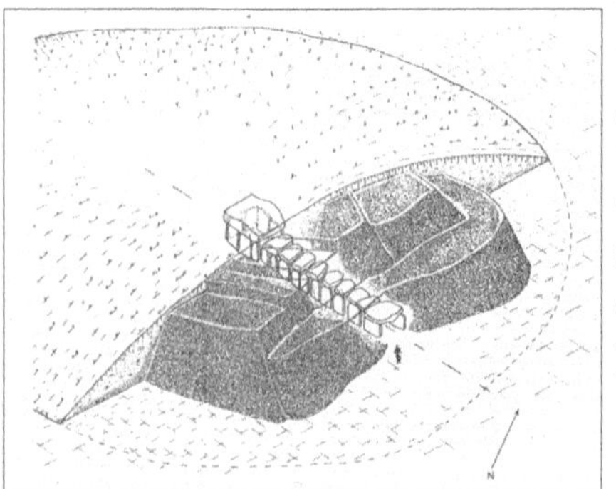
The cairn in cross section

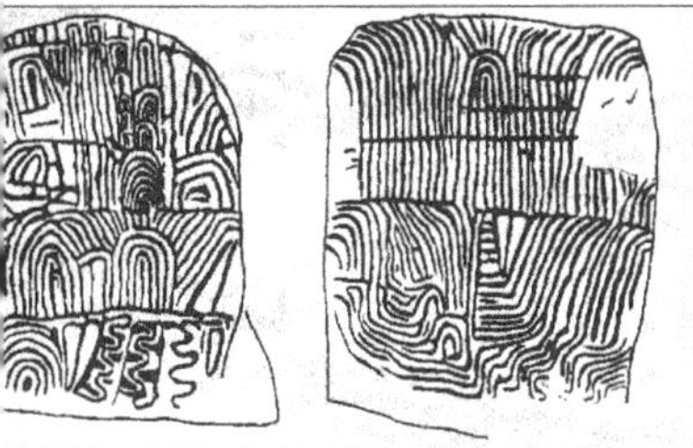

Typical carved stones in Gavrinis

and shines onto the far wall.

Apparently Gavrinis was suddenly abandoned around 3000 BCE. In front of the tumulus there had been a wooden structure, which was burnt down. It is thought that ceremonies were held there. After it was burnt, stones were piled up to block the entrance. Sand was laid on top, hiding the entrance—and the nature of the cairn itself. It was only rediscovered in 1835.

The interior of the tumulus is breathtaking. Of the fifty rough-hewn stone slabs that make up the dolmen, 23 of the supporting stones are prodigiously carved—and what carvings these are. The engravings are stunning and mysterious, and their cumulative effect makes Gavrinis one of the great wonders of the world—and not just the megalithic world. Crooks, interlaced U signs, axes in the shape of elongated triangles, shields, anthropomorphic deities, fingerprint whorls, snakes, zigzags, arrows, spirals—for the most part, the names we give to these designs says more about us than about their original meanings. The extensive carvings were made by pecking at the stones with tiny quartz pebbles.

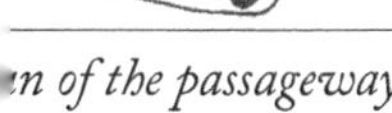

n of the passageway

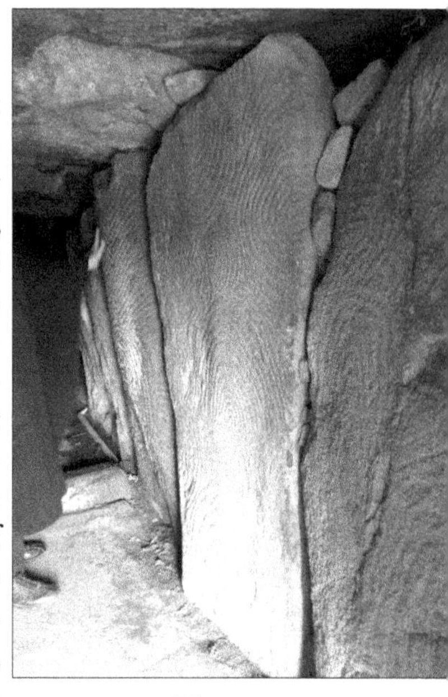

The passageway

But why? What was the purpose of this elaborately decorated gallery, burrowing long and straight into the center of the earthen mound? Scholars speculate that many of the carvings are schematic representations of the Mother Goddess. Perhaps it *embodied* the Goddess. If so, perhaps important ceremonies took place when the winter solstice sunrise penetrated the vaginal-like entrance to the Mother's womb.

And what was the purpose of the decorated slab in the inner chamber that has three deep holes leading to a recessed niche? Geologists claim they are naturally occurring holes—but even so, that stone was chosen and placed there for a reason. Again, we'll probably never know. And we'll also probably never know why the cairn was so abruptly closed, its ceremonial use so decisively terminated.

Elyn Aviva

Sign at the port in Larmor-Baden

Area map

Although it is difficult to get a sense of the interior of Gavrinis when you are on a twenty-minute-long visit with twenty other people (the maximum admitted at one time), it is still possible to sense the power of the place. All around you are elaborately carved stones covered with curving and swirling and straight lines. The designs can be appreciated aesthetically, but the challenge is to experience them "energetically." What do you think they might mean? How does the passageway feel to you? *What* does it feel like to you? Imagine walking into the darkness with only an oil lamp; imagine waiting for the sun's rays to pierce the darkness.

By the way, as you sail to Gavrinis, don't miss the tiny island of Er Lanic, just south of Gavrinis. Depending on the tides, you should be able to see two cromlechs forming a figure eight, half-submerged in the sea. The sea level was lower when they were erected, and

Elyn Aviva

Approach to Gavrinis

one could walk from Er Lanic to Gavrinis—and to what is now the mainland.

More to Experience

Don't miss the Île aux Moines in the Gulf of Morbihan, the largest island in the gulf. The Isle of the Monks has been inhabited since Neolithic times and has several megalithic sites, including the largest cromlech in France, at Kergonan, and, to the south, the dolmens of Pen-Hap and Boglieux. As the name suggests, the island was a former monastic fief. The island's forests have evocative names: Bois d'Amour (Wood of Love), Bois des Regrets (Wood of Regrets), and Bois des Soupirs (Wood of Sighs). The microclimate gives this island a very particular feeling, and it is a quiet seaside resort (except in high season), with attractive seventeenth- and eighteenth-century houses. Ferries depart from Port-Blanc or Vannes-Conleau. See www.izenah-croisiers.com or www.compagniedesiles.com (among others) for information.

Getting There

Although Gulf of Morbihan cruises sail by the island and give you a tantalizing view of the cairn, the only way to get to Gavrinis is by a fifteen-minute-long boat ride from Larmor-Baden, between March and November. The ticket cost includes

Leaving Gavrinis

the boat ride and the guided tour (about 50 minutes, part of which is outside the cairn). Even if you were to arrive on Gavrinis by private yacht, you could not get inside the cairn without a guide.

Call +33 02 97 57 19 38 to check on the schedule; it is advisable to reserve tickets, especially during high season. Contact gavrinis@sagemor.fr or go to www.gavrinis.info and www.patrimoine-morbihan.info. Although the guided tour is in French, some of the tour guides speak some English. The information plaques outside the cairn are also interesting, and they are translated into English. (Don't forget to use your "Pass des Mégalithes" for a discount.)

It is possible that visitors will be barred from the site in the future because of the damage that has been done to the site.

To get the ferry to Gavrinis, go to Larmor-Baden, eight miles south of Auray. Take D101 from Auray. Turn on D316 at Baden toward Larmor-Baden. Look for signs for the port.

Notes

Elyn Aviva

Miraculous spring of Ste-Anne-d'Auray

Basilique Ste-Anne (St. Anne Basilica), Auray

It began with the apparition of Anne, the mother of the Virgin, one dark and foggy August night in the year 1623. Or maybe it wasn't foggy. At any rate, Ste Anne appeared to the devout, illiterate Breton ploughman, Yves Nicolazic, and told him to rebuild her chapel, which had been destroyed 924 years and 6 months earlier. She was quite precise. Two years later a candle flame led Nicolazic to the statue of Anne buried in a nearby field. Brittany's most important pilgrimage site began as a ghost story—or rather, as the story of an apparition.

A Breton friend told us that some Bretons believe Ste Anne was once the queen of Brittany (probably confusing her with Anne of Brittany, who lived at the turn of the sixteenth century). He *knows Ste Anne's is* really *a shrine to Anna, the Mother Goddess, not to the Christian saint. (Elyn)*

Just north of Auray is the most popular pilgrimage shrine in Brittany, second in France only to Lourdes. Some 800,000 visitors/pilgrims come to the shrine each year. The *Grand Pardon* on July 26 is a spectacular event, with as many as 25,000 spectators and a long procession of priests and pilgrims. Participants carry elaborate banners of embroidered silk and sing Hail Marys and Breton hymns after the Mass.

The *pardon* originated with the discovery in 1625 of a very crude statue by a local peasant, Yves Nicolazic. He claimed that in 1623 Ste Anne appeared to him and, over the next few years, demanded that her church, which she said had been destroyed some 900 years earlier, be rebuilt. She appeared to him several times, asserting (in Breton), "God wants me to be honored in this place," and "I chose this site by liking."

At first the report of the illiterate, Breton-speaking farmer was greeted with skepticism. On the evening of March 7, 1625, however, the statue of Ste Anne was miraculously discovered where she had told Nicolazic it would be found, and skepticism turned to belief. But not for the entire ecclesiastic establishment. As Nicolazic lay dying twenty years later, the clergy was still interrogating him. By then the church had been built (or rebuilt, if you believed in the apparition), and popular devotion was unstoppable. Nicolazic's supporters (including the Bishop of Vannes) sided with the Breton farmer; the nobility and clergy continued to doubt. Obviously this was (and still remains) a case of religious politics and politicized religion.

"Perhaps, after all, the Earth does h
bor spirits—or there is something
the nature of certain places that
interact with the mind to produce
sual imagery of a characteristic ki
Paul Devereux, *Re-Visioning the Ea*
p. 219.

The nineteenth-century neo-Renaissance basilica is solemn and imposing, part of an impressive complex of monuments and memorials, including the Monument aux Morts erected by subscription to memorialize the 250,000 Bretons who died in World War I. Nearby is a National Necropolis, a cemetery for the dead from

"Rigid beliefs produce a rigid definition of reality. But in practice and in experience reality is fluid, because of the paradox 'Things have not only to be seen to be believed, but also to be believed to be seen.'" Tom Graves, *Needles of Stone Revisited*, p. 98.

Chapel dedicated to Ste Anne d'Auray

all wars since 1870. The Scala Sancta, an open-air chapel with a double set of stairs that devout pilgrims climb on their knees, is in the huge square in front of the basilica. A miraculous fountain flows in the center of the square, its large basin topped with a statue of Ste Anne and Mary (see p. 66). The town itself is drab, but it has a few more Ste-Anne-themed locations, including various large statues of Anne, the restored house of Nicolazic, and a wax museum with dioramas depicting the apparitions.

So why bother going to Ste-Anne's, aside from its popularity? Because of the apparition and the holy well, located at the site where Nicolazic was watering his cattle when the Lady appeared to him in 1623. Because a Breton friend said that Ste-Anne's is really a shrine to the Mother Goddess. Because a mysterious candle flame led Nicolazic and his neighbors to the field where the basilica now stands;

Elyn Aviva

Modern statue of Ste Anne d'Auray

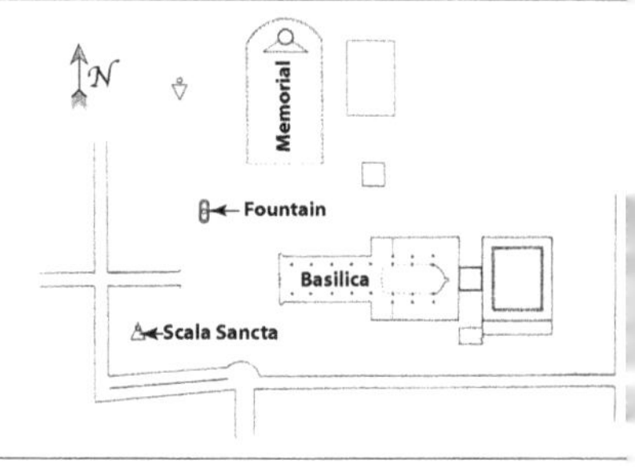

Site plan

there, they discovered the ancient statue, apparently where the earlier chapel had stood. Where there's candle smoke there's fire—or in this case, when so many people are drawn to a place, there must be something there. And something there was.

It is now thought that in the fifth or sixth century, missionaries constructed a chapel to Ste Anne at that location.This chapel was destroyed in the year 700. Although the hamlet was known as Ker Anna, it is highly unlikely that Nicolazic was privy to its history. Besides, the existence and location of the chapel had been long forgotten. And none of that explains the apparition or the candle flame. Earth-mysteries researcher Paul Devereux finds a correlation between fault lines (which there are under the basilica) and the occurrence of unusual, usually globular, lights (see grey box below). What Nicolazic and friends saw, or thought they saw, was candle light, but perhaps they "saw" candlelight because that's the kind of light they knew.

> "It is my firm opinion, based on research and direct experience of the phenomena, that the lights are an energy expression of the Earth Field. . . . Of all the possible interfaces between human and planetary consciousness, I suggest that earth lights are the most direct." Paul Devereux, *Earth Memory - Sacred Sites—Doorways into Earth's Mysteries,* p. 283.

Elyn found Ste-Anne's to be an unsettling shrine, a strange mix of over-the-top devotion and sincere veneration. She found the basilica itself energetically unbalanced. Gary dowsed a number of water lines and "fire" lines inside the basilica, perhaps accounting for Elyn's experience. Gary also found a powerful vortex in Ste Anne's chapel, in the south arm of the transept, in front of the altar. Our general impression was that there was lots of energy swirling around in the basilica, especially in Ste Anne's chapel. It wasn't chaotic but it was very active. Gary said it felt like being really close to Niagara Falls.

"Place is not passive. It interacts with our consciousness in a dynamic way. It contains its own memory of events and its own mythic nature, its *genius loci* or spirit of place, which may not be visible but can be apprehended by the human—and animal—interloper, especially in the appropriate mental state... ." Paul Devereux, *Re-Visioning the Earth*, p. 88.

The presence of the vortex made us wonder if this was the location of the original chapel or, perhaps where the buried statue was found. We have no idea how the powerful energy of the place relates to the apparitions, but it seems likely that the energy was there first and the chapel was built where the energy was. We think our Breton friend was right, and before the Christians built their chapel to Anne, mother of the Virgin, the Celtic Earth Mother Anna was worshipped at that powerful place.

According to Jean Markale, veneration of Ste Anne didn't begin in the Roman Catholic Church until the fourteenth century (*The Great Goddess*, pp. 150-151). (Although he doesn't say so, veneration had begun in the sixth century in the Eastern Orthodox Church). If Markale is right, it is even less likely that the crude statue was of Ste Anne. Perhaps the site where it was found was the remains of a Celtic sacred site dedicated to Anna—and hence the hamlet's name, Ker Anna. Perhaps later a chapel was built on the site, effectively "christening" it "Ste Anne" in honor of the mother of the mother of Jesus—thus continuing the veneration of the Mother Goddess at the same location. Markale asserts: "Now, in all Celtic countries, Saint Anne is the Christian transposition of Dana-Anna of ancient mythology, the mother of the gods and of men" (p. 128).

Perhaps what Nicolazic experienced was the spiritual nature of the place, the *genius loci* (or perhaps the *anima loci,* the "place-soul")— urging him to remember the sacredness of the land, reminding him to have

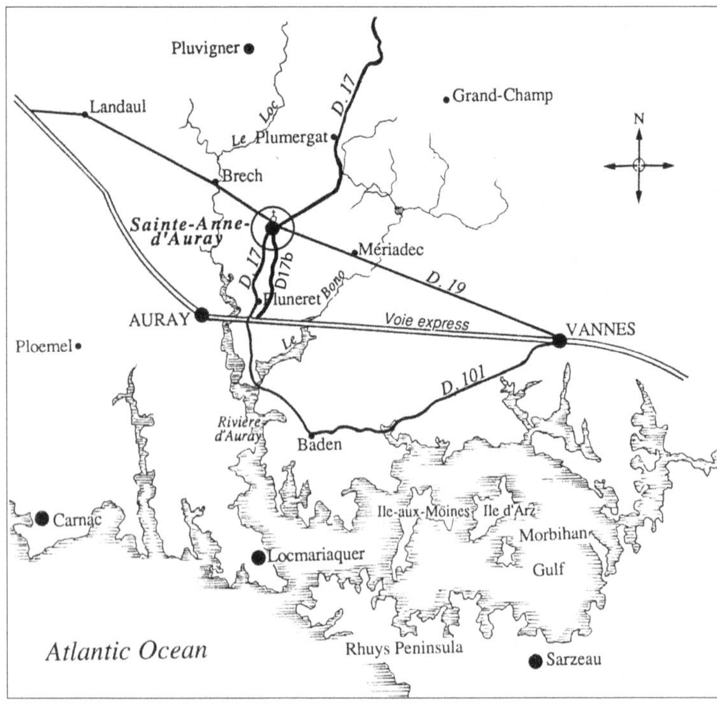

Area map

a personal relationship with (as Nigel Pennick puts it) "the goddess of the landscape, who is Mother Earth in her local form" *(Celtic Sacred Landscapes,* p. 7).

If you go to Ste-Anne-d'Auray—preferably not during the *Grand Pardon* on July 26, when the town is extremely crowded—see what you experience and let us know if you have any insights.

Getting There

Ste-Anne-d'Auray is four miles north of Auray via D17 and fourteen miles northwest of Vannes. Leave Vannes on N165-E60 west. Exit on D17b to Sainte-Anne-D'Auray.

Notes

Elyn Aviva

Chapelle Ste-Barbe from the woods below

Chapelle Ste-Barbe (St. Barbe's Chapel), near Le Faouët

The guidebook said Saint Barbe's church was a difficult place to reach, built on the side of a nearly inaccessible cliff overlooking the Ellé River. But we had no difficulty. Perhaps the road has changed. We parked at the top of the cliff and walked over to the bell tower (ring it for good luck) and St Michel's oratory. We followed the steps down to Ste-Barbe's, admiring the chapel but more interested in her holy well. Down we went and down, following a narrow trail through the forest, verdant and vibrant with hints of faeries and elementals. Soon we reached the holy well, covered by a structure built in 1708. We knew the sacred spring was much older, older than Christian claims to its fame. Perhaps the "original" Ste Barbe was older, too—perhaps she was an elemental goddess connected with fire.... (Elyn)

Ste Barbe's legend is intriguing, in part because it hints at things not said, stories not told. One source (see http://63.249.123.11/neu/celt/lrb/lrb15.htm and http://www.sacred-texts.com/neu/celt/lrb/lrb15.htm) claims that Ste Barbe is "one of the strangest and most 'pagan' of the Breton saints. She protects those who seek her aid from sudden death, especially death by lightning. In recent years, popular belief has extended her sphere of influence to cover those who travel by automobile! She is also regarded as the patroness of firemen, at whose annual dinner her statue, surrounded by flowers, presides."

The legend tells us that Ste Barbe was so beautiful that her pagan father locked her in a tower (shades of Rapunzela). Nonetheless, she communicated with

Chapelle Ste-Barbe seen from above

Origen of Alexandria and asked him to teach her about Christianity. Supposedly, he sent a monk to instruct her and she became Christian. To punish her for her conversion, the Gallo-Roman pro-consul had her beaten and forced her to walk naked through the streets. However, the Christian god heard her prayers, and a "cloud descended and hid her from the gaze of the impious mortals…." It looked as if she would be saved when she was spirited away to a mountaintop, but her father learned where she was from a shepherd and beheaded her. As punishment, her father was struck by lightning and the shepherd was turned into marble. Or so goes the legend. Whatever the truth, Ste Barbe is a powerful, miracle-working saint, often associated with lightning and fire—and preservation from sudden death.

Elyn Aviva

Statue of Ste Barbe in the chapel tower

The origin of the chapel dates to the mid-fifteenth century, when the Lord of Toulboudou was out hunting. He encountered a terrible thunderstorm and could find no shelter. His huntsmen "trembled for their lives, and doubtless repeated with much fervor the old Breton charm," which, roughly translated, is:

"Saint Barbe the great and sainted Clair,
Preserve me from the lightning's glare.
When thunderbolts are flashing red
Let them not burst upon my head."

The Lord of Toulboudou vowed to build a chapel in Ste Barbe's honor on the cliff above—if she saved him from death. "No sooner had he made this vow than the storm subsided, and safety was once more assured." The archive at Le Faouët records that "on the 6th of July, 1489, John of Toulboudou bought of John of Bouteville, Lord of Faouët, a piece of ground on the flank of the Roche-Marche-Bran, twenty-five feet by sixteen feet, on which to build a chapel to the honor of St Barbe, and there the chapel stands to this day."

Postage stamp of Ste Barbe

Her annual *pardon* on the last Sunday of June is very popular. Pilgrims purchase *Couronnes de Ste Barbe* amulets, believed to protect against sudden death.

Chapelle Ste-Barbe is located in a cleft on the side of a hill, 300 feet above the Ellé Valley. The view is impressive. The chapel is not the only construction, however. The Oratoire St-Michel (Saint Michael Oratory) is built out on a spur of rock above, near a small gazebo-like bell-tower, and

Bell tower

pilgrims ring the bell for blessings. (It is not as easy to ring the bell as one might think: you really have to work for your blessing!) A staircase of 78 steps, built in 1700, leads down to the chapel dedicated to Ste Barbe. It was closed when we were there, but from the outside, Gary dowsed a water line running down the nave and an earth or "fire" line outside the east wall.

A trail leads down from Ste Barbe's chapel into the valley, through the green and rustling forest to the holy well, and then to the Ellé River. The sacred spring is about a five- to eight-minute walk from the chapel. Walking through the forest, we felt as if we had entered into a magical land filled with joyous, welcoming life-force. The spring is reputed to have healing pow-

Elyn Aviva

Oratoire St-Michel

The holy well

ers and draws many pilgrims. That isn't surprising, given the energy that we felt in the forest.

It is most probable that the healing well dates from long before Ste Barbe—just as Ste Barbe is likely a Christianized version of a pagan goddess. Could she be related to Celtic Brigit, goddess of the hearth, healing, smithing, poetry, and the perpetual sacred fire (as well as high-rising flames, high places, and hillsides)? The *genius loci* of this location is very strong. Perhaps the mixture of fervent faith and the spirit of the place itself contributed to saving the Lord of Toulboudou and his faithful huntsmen.

Nineteenth-century drawing of the well

More to Experience

Le Faouët has a sixteenth-century covered market with a slate roof, a museum of nineteenth-century paintings, and a bee museum. Near Le Faouët are two other chapels, St-Nicolas and St-Fiacre. St-Fiacre is two miles southeast of Le Faouët and has a lovely, lace-like, fifteenth-century rood screen, designed to separate the chancel from the congregation. Its carved wooden panels are unusual, depicting (among other things) a man vomiting a fox. Also in the vicinity is Kernascléden, with its fifteenth-century church containing fine frescoes, including a powerful Dance of Death.

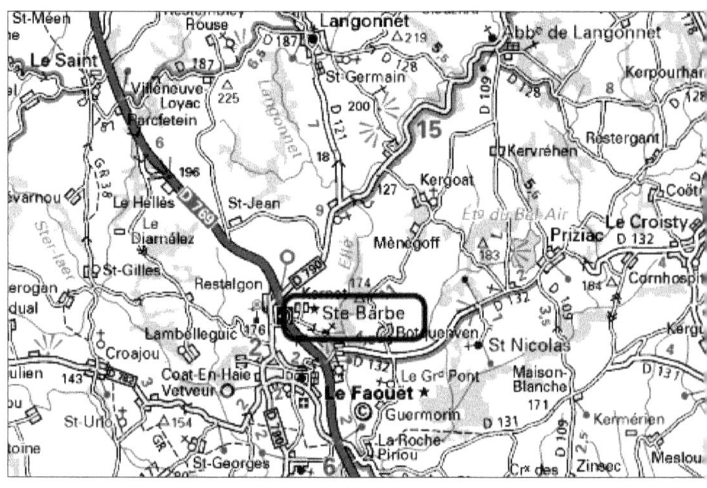

Area map

Getting There

Chapelle Ste-Barbe is 1.8 miles northeast of Le Faouët on D790. Le Faouët can be reached from Lorient going north on D769. Look for signs to D790 and continue north.

Notes

Elyn Aviva

Vénus de Quinipily with fountain and trough below

La Vénus de Quinipily (The Venus of Quinipily), near Baud

I don't know what she is, this towering, crudely carved female statue. A colossal joke? A poorly sculpted effigy? A peculiar piece of oversized garden statuary? "They" say she is an ancient goddess statue, transported and placed on top of a pedestal above a sacred spring. "They" say she is Egyptian, but it's hard to know. "They" say she was obscene, the focus of pagan fertility rites. Tossed into the nearby river several times and rescued, she was recarved to make a more modest presentation. Or so they say. Her secrets, if any there were, remain secure. Disappointed, I walk back down the path, then turn for one last look. I think I see her shift upon her pedestal and smile. (Elyn)

The Vénus de Quinipily is a granite statue, over seven feet high, perched on top of a pedestal over a fountain with a large trough, also made of granite. Both the statue and the trough were moved together from their original location. Until the seventeenth century, the statue and the trough were located in Bieuzy-les-Eaux, on the hill of Castennec, where the Gallic city of Sulim was founded. Don't expect the statue's current spot to be a powerful place, although the lovely gardens and the ruined château are quite evocative.

Regardless of her "nouveaux" setting, the Venus herself is quite intriguing. Almost naked, rough carved, some think she represents Isis, the Egyptian goddess whose cult spread through the Mediterranean with the Romans. Known by local Bretons as "the Iron Lady" or "the Old Guardian," the statue was worshipped by peasants—or at least, that's what the Bishop of Vannes feared they were doing. One source says

Château de Quinipily in 1776

that young women asked the Venus for help in finding lovers, and older women asked for safe childbirth. Perhaps other fertility requests were more overt. In 1661 the Bishop had the statue thrown into the Blavet River. But in 1664 the peasants pulled her out of the river and began their "pagan rituals" once again. In 1670 the Bishop had the statue mutilated (is that when her breasts were chiseled down?) and again thrown into the river. In 1695, Pierre de Lannion, Governor of Vannes, recovered the statue and had it placed in its new location at his castle of Quinipily, turning the cult statue into a piece of garden statuary. Or so it seemed, although devotees continued to visit the statue into the late eighteenth century.

Some archeologists think the Venus is a statue of Isis, worshipped by the Roman legions that settled in Sulim after defeating the Gauls; others, that it is Cybele, a Gallic goddess. Others claim that this is a new statue, carved

Vénus de Quinipily

Nineteenth-century drawing of the Vénus de Quinipily

to replace the old. Given that there was a protracted court battle over which of two aristocrats was the rightful owner of the "retrieved" statue, it's doubtful it was just a copy.

It is unclear when the name Venus became associated with the statue; perhaps the name reflects its long association with love and fertility. There is evidence of a widespread Venus cult during the Roman era.

We find it curious that the Venus statue was considered so threatening that it was "drowned" several times—once, after being mutilated. Wouldn't it have been easier to simply hack it into bits? Maybe there was more power residing in her stony form than the authorities were willing to admit. Although she is no longer in her original setting (which was, perhaps, a powerful place), she is still associated with the granite water trough. Is there a link between these two, regardless of locale? The trough is made out of a granite monolith—was it a menhir, once upon a time? The mystery thickens.

If you follow the trail on either side of the Venus that leads into the higher gardens, you'll reach a little shrine with a statue of St Michel stabbing a horned

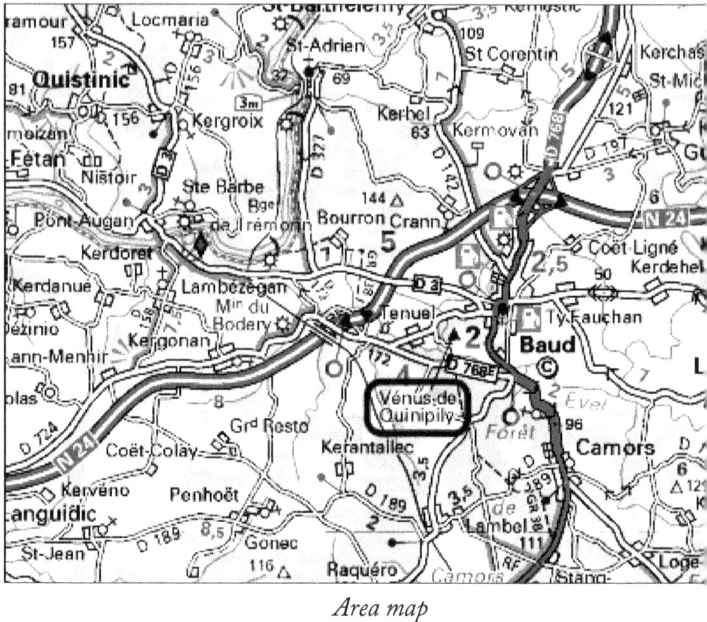

Area map

devil with carbuncles on his rear. In front of the shrine is a pool with a tiny menhir in the middle. Does this landscape feature hint at something hidden? Probably not. Probably it is just an example of meaningful symbols—and megalithic stones—being turned into meaningless decoration. We wouldn't say the same about the Venus of Quinipily, however. Power seems to reside in her still.

More to Experience

The Fôret de Camors is nearby. Trails lead to several impressive menhirs. In the center, where the paths meet at the Étoile (the "star"), is a massive oak tree.

Getting There

The gardens and château of Quinipily are about two km (one mile) southwest of Baud. Turn onto D768E

south of Baud to go to Tenuel. Just past Tenuel, follow the road sign on the right to the Vénus de Quinipily. There is a €3 entrance fee.

To reach the gardens from Ste-Barbe, return to Lorient on D769 and at Lanester continue on D724 to the east. Take N165/E60 towards Vannes and exit to N24 and then to D724 towards Baud. Watch for signs to the Vénus de Quinipily.

To explore the Fôret de Camors, go south of Baud on D768 in the direction of Auray.

Notes

Yann Caradec

Pointe St-Mathieu, Finistère

Around Finistère

Sometimes divided into Northern and Southern Finistère, this is the Land's End of France, the region furthest west. For centuries these two regions looked to Grand Bretagne (Great Britain) instead of "Petite Bretagne" (Brittany). Northern Finistère is also known as Léon, corresponding to ancient Lyonesse, and further subdivided into upper, which features intensive agriculture, and lower, which is much less developed. Southern Finistère corresponds to the historic kingdom of Cornouaille (Cornwall). This is the homeland of Tristan, whose star-crossed love for Isolde led to ruin. Centuries ago, Finistère was the last refuge of the Druids fleeing the inexorable spread of Christianity. Finistère remains steeped in Arthurian memories, traditional customs, and deep religiosity. Today it is considered by some to be the spiritual heartland of Brittany—no longer pagan but devoutly Breton Catholic.

Stretching east-west between Northern and Southern Finistère lie the Parc Naturel Régional d'Amorique and the legend-drenched Monts d'Arrée. The Monts d'Arrée's highest "peak" is 1260 feet, but everything is relative. The Monts cover 148,000 acres and form the hilly spine of Finistère. Sparsely populated, for centuries the area has been rich with legends and tales of sorcery—perhaps due to the peculiar nature of the land itself. Hills, marshes, peat bogs, granite, and rare wildlife all contribute to give the region a very particular atmosphere.

The "End of the World" is an isolated, remote, rural landscape, full of powerful places. Wild coastline, picturesque *rias* or *abers* (estuaries), elaborate parish closes, traditional festivals, megalithic sites, isolated islands, attractive cities, and remote hills make it worth exploring.

A calvary in a parish close

Although it's never visible, the church bells of the legendary kingdom of Ys can sometimes be heard—according to sailors. Ys (or Is) lies lost in the Baie de Douarnenez, off the west coast of the Crozon peninsula. On Crozon you also find rugged Ménez-Hom, a "mountain" held to be sacred by the Celts and today considered the land of the *korrigans* and elves. There are megaliths on the peninsula as well, for example, the Alignements de Lagatjar, between Camaret and Pointe du Tour-linguet.

Finistère

The town of Locronan is purported to have been a cen-

rnenez cairn, built around 4500 BCE, the largest and oldest in Europe

ter for Celtic Christianity 2500 years ago. It is now the location of an annual procession, the *Petite Tromènie*, on the second Sunday of July. Costumed devotees follow a route to the top of the nearby hill that may have originated as the fifth-century Irish St Ronan's Sunday walk. The every-six-year *Grand Tromènie* is an extended 7.5 mile circuit that may follow the stations of the Cross, or a Druid astronomical circuit, or a pre-Christian circuit of megalithic sites.

Some five miles off the Pointe du Raz (the most western point of France), Île de Sein has been inhabited since prehistoric times. According to a Roman source, nine virgin priestesses served a shrine on the island. It was also reputed to have been the last refuge of the Druids in Brittany, pushed offshore by the relentlessly ever-westward spread of Christianity.

There is much to see in this region. It warrants an extended stay—and perhaps a guidebook of its own. In this guidebook, however, we have limited ourselves to describing three of the many powerful places you can encounter in Finistère.

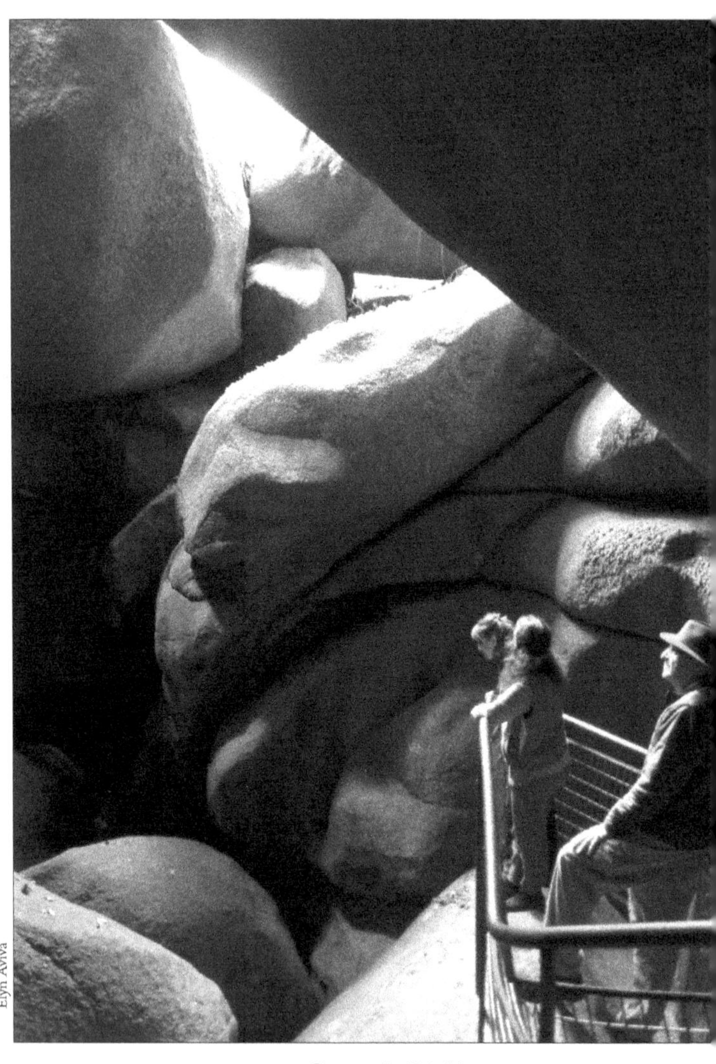
Elyn Aviva

Grotte du Diable

Forêt de Huelgoat (Forest of Huelgoat)

The forest is part of what little remains of the primeval forest that covered most of Brittany. Near the edge of town, at the Moulin du Chaos (Chaos Mill—how aptly named), we cross a bridge over the River Argent and leave the orderly urban life behind. Hundreds of immense, tumbled granite boulders lie piled helter-skelter on all sides. We are Lilliputians in the land of Giants. Following a well-marked trail alongside the glittering stream, we descend slowly and carefully into The Devil's Grotto, water rushing and swirling all around. The sound is impressive. Looking for a quieter experience, we hike on trails over hills and through the beechwood forest to the Cave of Arthur, where a fabulous treasure supposedly lies buried. There is much more to be discovered on another day, with a better map. (Elyn)

Huelgoat (from Breton "Uhel-Coat" or "High Forest") is a small town (population 1700), a popular base for hikers and anglers who fish in the lake and the River Argent (Silver River). The lake was created between the sixteenth and eighteenth centuries to supply water for the nearby silver and lead mining operations. Today, Huelgoat is one of the main "green tourism" attractions in Brittany. It is a pretty setting, with the lake at one edge of the town, the river, hiking trails that begin at the north edge of town, and a nearby botanical park. The Forêt de Huelgoat is located north and east of the village in the regional park known as the Parc Naturel Régional d'Armorique. A hurricane did tremendous damage to the forest in October 1987, smashing much of it beyond recognition, but over the decades it has been greatly restored.

Walking between granite boulders in

Surprisingly, you don't have to walk far to enter into a wonderland of hundreds of massive boulders and rushing water. Cross the bridge at the Moulin du Chaos and you enter a fascinating landscape filled with immense, moss-covered granite boulders, some balancing precariously on each other, others burrowed deeply into the tree-covered hillsides. Some of the boulders have picturesque names like the Roche Tremblante (Balancing Rock) and the Ménage de la Vierge (The Virgin's Household).

Elyn Aviva

Trail markers

A short distance down the well-marked trail is La Grotte du Diable, a grotto formed by a pile of huge boulders. You can follow slippery steps (use the handrail) and descend a ladder to the grotto and the subterranean river, 30 feet below. Be careful: it's somewhat peril-

The trail through the forest

ous, but it's worth it. You'll be standing right in front of a powerful waterfall. Although it's called The Devil's Cave, the energy inside felt feminine and womb-like—but fierce.

It is pleasant to spend a day strolling through the beechwood forest, gaining a sense of the great primeval forest that once covered inland Brittany. There are several interconnecting trails of varied lengths, so you can decide how much of a hike to take.

The Promenade du Fer à Cheval and Le Gouffre is a picturesque walk along the river. It leads to a chasm and to a lookout point with a commanding view. It continues on to La Mare aux Fées (The Fairy Pond). A local legend states that you can see faeries bathing in this pond by moonlight—but during the day, they turn into hideous witches. Supposedly, a faery was thrown into the pond as punishment and drowned.... Re-

Elyn Aviva

Grotte d'Artus (for scale, note person in shadow in center-right)

gardless of the "anti-faery" thrust of the legend, it is an indication of the enchanted nature of the forest.

The Promenade du Canal follows along the banks of the upper of two canals, dug in the nineteenth century for silver and lead mining operations. The Romans had already begun mining the lead, millennia ago. Another walk is the Promenade du Clair-Ruisseau, which leads to the Camp d'Artus and the Grotte d'Artus (Arthur's Cave), a Gallo-Roman fortified site rumored to contain buried Arthurian treasure. The cave is unexpectedly large. We found an intriguing carving on a nearby boulder—but no treasure.

Don't miss buckwheat *galettes* or drinks at the Crêperie de la Roche Tremblante, at the foot of the hill close to the Balancing Rock. It has a lovely, sunny garden. (Hours vary, and it is not open year around.)

Although there are descriptive placards at various points and signposts for the trails, we highly recommend that you have a good map with you. One is available at the tourist office, but that office has somewhat limited hours. It would be good to come prepared. See http://huelgoat.net/ and http://www.mareauxfees.com/huelgoat/ in English.

Elyn Aviva

Rock carving near Grotte d'Artus

More to Experience

Huelgoat is in the region known as the Monts d'Arrée, the hilly area between Léon and Cornouaille. This area is

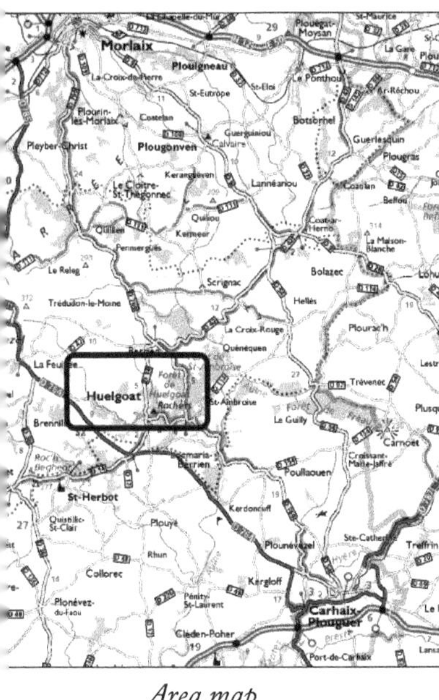

Area map

sparsely populated and contains spectacular landscapes filled with legends, enchantment, and mystery. It is also a nature sanctuary of sorts. If you have time, tour the region, stopping at the Vale of Yeun Elez (southwest of La Feuillée) to see the marshland (a "Gateway to Hell," according to local legends), the peat bogs of Saint-Michel-en-Rivoal, and the bare peaks of Roc'h Tredudon and Roc'h Trévézel. Our sense of the region was that it did not let us in easily. Let us know what you experience. See http://www.lesmontsdarree.fr/ for additional information.

> cording to Sergio Berti's extensive geobiophysical research, the ıelgoat area contains a number of interesting geological features, luding granite, sedimentary rocks, and numerous faults "that are e to reduce the sympathetic activity in people. These secondary lts have the tendency to cross." He links specific features with pop- r legends. See http://www.architetturageobiologia.it/home.html

Getting There

Huelgoat and the forest are located between Morlaix and Carhaix on D769.

Elyn Aviva

Statue of Salaün, the fool, exterior of the Basilique de Notre-Dame

Basilique de Notre-Dame (Basilica of Our Lady), Le Folgoët

It's named after a fool of the woods (fol goad), *a fool for love—a fool who dangled from trees in the forest and spent his life calling on the Virgin—"Ave María, Ave María" he muttered incessantly. He died and people soon learned who the real fool was: a lily grew from his grave, bearing the words "Ave María," writ in gold. And the fool's name? Salaün (Solomon). How sweet it feels inside the church, so calm and centering, as if the fool's love still permeates the atmosphere. I could stay here for an afternoon, a day, a week. A holy well (the fool's favorite spring) issues from under the altar; the fountain is outside, and pilgrims come to take the miraculous water. (Elyn)*

The village is small, the basilica impressive, and the annual *grand pardon* one of the biggest in Brittany. But what is it that draws people to Le Folgoët, far off the beaten path in Northern Finistère?

For one thing, the fifteenth-century basilica is magnificent. The north tower is one of the finest bell towers in Brittany, and the fifteenth-century carved granite rood screen is a masterpiece of Breton art. The stained glass is lovely, the fifteenth-century granite statue of Our Lady of Folgoët charming, and the statues that adorn the outside of the basilica range from amusing to moving.

Elyn Aviva

Exterior of the Basilique

Drawing of the fool and his grave

But there's a lot more here than that. We could start with the legend of a fool who praised the Virgin Mary deeply and sincerely, with his entire being. He was ridiculed by the villagers, but it didn't matter—he was a Divine Fool, brought closer, perhaps, in his "foolishness" to direct contact with Spirit—or at any rate, the Spirit of the Place. He lived alone in the forest, calling on (and perhaps seeing) the Virgin; he was found dead one day in 1358 (the date makes this story seem more real and less legend) near his favorite spring in the woods. But it wasn't until a lily sprouted from his neglected grave, miraculously bearing the golden letters "Ave María," that the villagers realized how holy—and how wise—the fool had really been.

Salaün is represented in several stained-glass windows, swinging from a tree near the spring—the very spring over which the basilica was erected. It should not go unnoticed that the spring where he spent his time and venerated the Mother is now considered a holy well—and probably was before Christianity came to this remote part of Brittany. Salaün's fountain on the outside of the east wall of

"How to apprehend place is possibly the greatest single lesson we have to learn from the archaic mind-set or worldview. We have to learn how to dream with open eyes. In terms of cognitive science, we will have to reprogram our neuronal processes to allow into the limelight of our consciousness the information received from place that currently falls outside the spectrum of our awareness." Paul Devereux, *Re-Visioning the Earth,* p. 101.

ained glass window in the Basilique

the church is fed by the spring that issues from under the altar. Sounds geomantically interesting, doesn't it?

The church felt sweet and centering, perhaps reflecting Salaün's life-long love affair with the Goddess. It is clearly well loved and well cared for by the community, as well as being an illustrious pilgrimage site. Spend time inside and see if you don't feel peaceful and "slowed down," the way we did. Gary dowsed a water line running down the nave—not surprising, since the spring issues from under the altar.

More to Experience

While you are exploring this northern part of Northern Finistère, don't miss visiting the fjord-like Côte des Abers, the Coast of the Estuaries. If you go further east, you can visit the region around Morlaix, perhaps basing yourself in Landivisiau. The parish closes of St-Thégonnec, Lampaul-Guimiliau, Guimil-

Elyn Aviva

The holy well on the east exterior

iau, and La Martyre are famous. They provide an intriguing insight into the Breton relationship with the dead. Ossuaries or charnel houses are found next to several of the churches, a pattern of "keeping the dead close" that some researchers think goes back to the megalith builders. Still farther east, along the coast, you can visit the 6500-year-old Cairn de Barnenez. It contains eleven dolmens and is considered the largest and oldest cairn in Europe.

"However we try to juggle the evidence to fit those various mo convenient theories, we are always brought back to that pagan so lution: that nature is intelligent, and is using people, through th forms that people in those siting-legends described as fairies, ange the Devil, or just 'something,' to help it maintain its energy-matri its nervous system, its veins and arteries. The sacred sites, as w have seen, are on node-points of the energy-matrix; and the stru tures at those sites were built where and how they are, and wi the extraordinary properties they show, not through analysis an logical systems, but because the builders understood and obeye that 'something' beyond them, through dreams, through divin tion, through 'coincidence,' through feelings." Tom Graves, *Needl of Stone Revisited*, pp. 172-173.

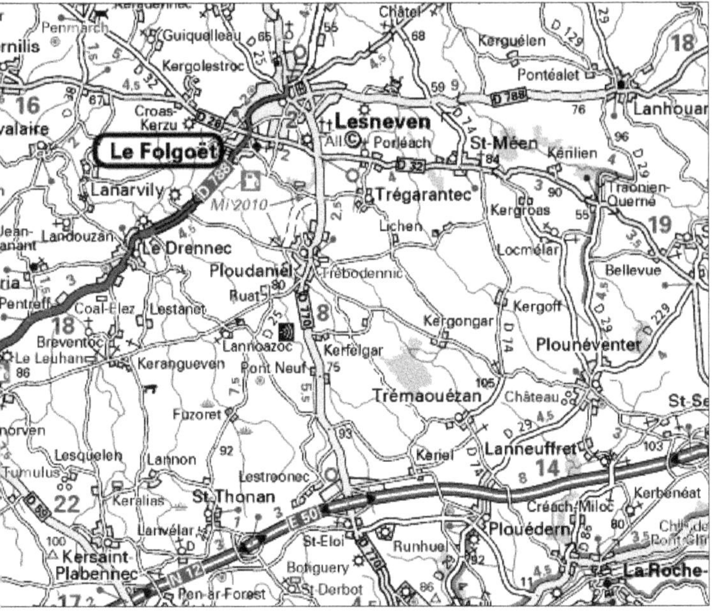

Area map

Getting There

Le Folgoët is thirteen miles north of Brest via D788. If you come from Morlaix, take E50 in the direction of Brest. Exit on D770 toward Lesneven. South of Lesneven exit on D32 to Le Folgoët.

Notes

Elyn Aviva

Cloister of Abbaye de Daoulas

Daoulas

What a delightful town: walking paths, a stream crossed by scenic bridges, fifteenth- and seventeenth-century row houses, still occupied. An old and "new" abbey with a large cemetery and covered porch. We paid a fee and entered the old abbey, admiring the reconstructed twelfth-century cloister, then wandered through the medicinal garden. Strolling around the park, we saw a healing well, an oratory, a strange priapic statue, giant rhubarb plants (also known as "dinosaur food"), with huge cone flowers and immense, curling leaves. A good place to come for a break from more serious investigations. (Elyn)

Sometimes being a tourist isn't such a bad thing, especially in a pleasant place like Daoulas. Daoulas is not without its more serious attractions, but they don't have to be taken too seriously. Stroll through town, enjoying the lovely bridges and paths around the river, then wend your way slowly (no rush, this is a vacation!) up the rue de l'Église from the center of town to visit the ancient abbey (admission fee).

Abbaye de Daoulas has had a checkered history, not unlike that of many other French religious buildings. It is possible that in 510 a monastery was built on the site of the murder of two abbots, but if so, nothing remains; perhaps it was destroyed or abandoned during the Norman invasions. The current abbey was founded in the

Elyn Aviva

The abbey church

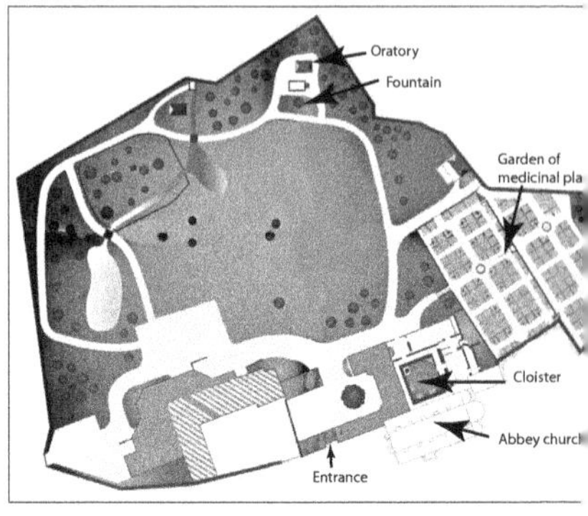

The abbey grounds

twelfth century and thrived for a number of centuries. But by the late eighteenth century it was in decline, and in 1790 it became a parish church. In 1792 the buildings became private property. The cloister stones were scattered and other buildings destroyed as the complex was adapted into living spaces for families, not monks.

In 1880 an attempt was made to restore what remained. In 1947 the Congregation of Franciscan Sisters of Blois bought what was left and built a primary school and later a convalescent home. In 1984 the Community sold the domain to the Finistère Regional Council. Now the buildings have been re-utilized once again, turning the abbey and its grounds into an international cultural center that stages "ambitious historical exhibitions," an extensive garden of medicinal plants, and a collection of restored and partly reconstructed buildings.

Elyn Aviva

The cloister

It has a certain charm. Even after so much misuse and re-use, the remains of the cloister are peaceful and quiet. The three sides that remain form the only Romanesque

The basin in the cloister

cloister in Brittany. A perfectly preserved twelfth-century ablutions basin covered with Celtic-style designs and masks bubbles and gurgles in one corner. The nearby Garden of Medicinal Plants is inspired by monastic gardens (containing medicinal, aromatic, and culinary plants) dating back to the Middle Ages, but it has been updated to include exotic and endangered species. The garden contains 400 species native to Brittany, Africa, and Oceania.

We strolled around the grounds, appreciating the botanical labels on a number of trees. The path led us to Notre-Dame-des-Fontaines, an oratory built in 1550. Inside on the right wall we saw a rare statue of Bishop Saint Théleau (or Thélo) riding a stag. According to legend, a day's journey on the stag delimited the territory of the bishop. Is this another hint of Cernunnos (see pp. 39-41)? Next to the oratory is Our Lady's Fountain, which has (or had) a reputation for treating eye disease and sterility. Once the waters ran clean, but now they are scummy and looked more likely to cause illness than to cure it.

Elyn Aviva

Bishop St Thélau

Elyn Aviva

Holy well at the oratory

To the left of the oratory is a most unusual, small, moss-covered statue. At first we thought it was a Sheela-na-gig (a statue of a female, usually skeletal, with her hands holding open her vagina), but then we realized that the figure was masculine and holding a very different anatomical part. Where the statue came from we were unable to determine, but it feels as if it was not just a piece of garden statuary.

Outside the abbey is the sixteenth-century parish close. It contains the abbey church, which still has its original Romanesque west door, nave, and north side aisle. The close has an elaborate Gothic porch, which leads into the cemetery. What was once the ossuary has been converted into a sacristy. Across the street is a charming chapel to Ste Anne.

The town is located on the banks of the Daoulas River, and a number of marked trails encourage the visitor to stroll both inside and outside of the town. See www.abbaye-daoulas.com or http://www.cheminsdupatrimoineenfinistere.com/daoulas-labbayeenbref.html.

Statue at the oratory

More to Experience

Continue south and east to the Monts d'Arrée—includ-

View of the river and the town

ing Huelgoat—or west to Plougastel-Daoulas (famous for strawberries and its parish close). If you continue a bit farther south to Southern Finistère, you can visit the Crozon Peninsula (megaliths, the sunken legendary kingdom of Ys, the sacred "mountain" Ménez-Hom, and Île de Sein. See pp. 90-91).

A little farther south is Quimper, purported to be the most Celtic city in Brittany. Brittany's oldest city (founded by Gauls), it was the capital of the ancient diocese, kingdom, and later duchy of Cornouaille. The first bishop of Quimper was St Corentin, who came across the Channel sometime between the fourth and seventh centuries. Legend says he had a most unusual diet, living by eating a regenerating and immortal fish—a legend filled with Celtic resonances. His mythic story relates to another, that of King Gradlon, king of the mythic drowned city of Ys (or Is). Saved by St Corentin, Gradlon went on to found Quimper—or so the time-askew legend goes. St Corentin cathedral is built on the site of a Roman temple.

For something completely different, consider attending the largest Breton festival in the world, the week-long Cornouaille Festival, which ends on the fourth Sunday in July. Filled with concerts, exhibitions, dance performances, traditional costumes, and Breton food, groups participate from other Celtic countries as well. See www.festival-cornouaille.com

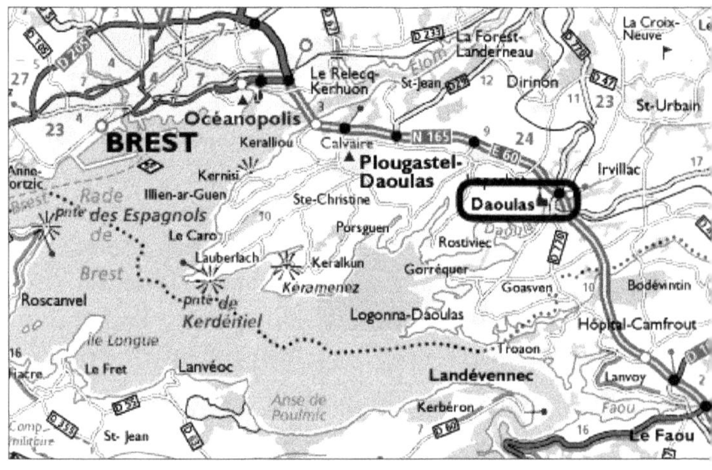

Area map

Getting There

Follow N165 between Brest and Quimper. Daoulas is 9 miles southeast of Brest and 31 miles north of Quimper.

Notes

Elyn Aviva

Abbaye de Paimpont from across the Étang de Paimpont

Around the Forêt de Brocéliande or de Paimpont (the Forest of Brocéliande or Paimpont)

It's not surprising that this area goes by different names. Some call it the Forest of Brocéliande; others call it the Forest of Paimpont. Paimpont exists on official maps—but Brocéliande is a state of mind. Within its borders, reality seems to shift a bit: myth becomes history, and the landscape resonates with Merlin's magic and King Arthur's memory. Where else but here would you find the (invisible) crystal palace that Merlin built for Vivian, the Lady of the Lake, in the lake next to a charming château? Or Merlin's tomb, disguised as a dynamited Neolithic dolmen? Or the effervescent Fountain of Barenton, where weather magic used to be worked? Or the Val sans Retour (Valley of No Return), where Morganna imprisoned unfaithful knights? Or the holy well of Ste Onenne in Tréhorenteuc, where healings actually *do* sometimes happen?

And there is more, much more. Brocéliande really *is* a "thin" place, where the veil between this world and the realm of Spirit is more easily crossed. A mixture of nature, geography, and legend come together to create a world filled with extraordinary trees, over fifty megalithic sites, lakes, streams, holy wells—and a church dedicated to the Grail.

Although all of this might sound like a lot of modern tourism hype, the association of the forest with Merlin began over eight hundred years ago. Brocéliande has been the location of Arthurian legends since long before the twelfth century. Based on Celtic mythology passed down on both sides of the Channel (don't forget—Brittany was "Little Britain"), the stories eventually were transformed into the romances about King Arthur and his knights. The Arthurian cycle became extremely popular and eventually incorporated not only Celtic mythology but also medieval Christian legends and the chivalric code. Although some might argue whether Brocéliande is really the forest described in these early tales, those who have spent time there have little doubt.

The Forêt de Brocéliande was once known as Brécelien, etymologically related to *Barc'h Helan,* the land of the Druids. It is what remains of the primeval forest that once covered much of Brittany. Logging in the forest (most is in private ownership) has reduced it today to 27 square miles; only 2 square miles belongs to the state. You won't notice this, though, as you follow the numerous hiking trails through the extensive stands of beech, chestnut, birch, alder, oak, and—increasingly—conifer. A devastating forest fire in 1990 destroyed much of the forest, but it has been replanted with evergreens, and gorse, heather, broom, and ferns thrive in the open places. The land itself is a mix of granite, red slate, and quartz, some of which juts out as evocative ridges on the hillsides. Ironworking was important here over 2000 years ago and continued until the late nineteenth century.

The Forest of Paimpont is 25 miles southwest of Rennes. Getting there by car is easy—but entering Brocéliande may take a little more doing. Or maybe not. Every time we've been there, strange synchronicities occur. We are enchanted with the forest—or perhaps it has enchanted us. The first time we went there, years ago, we stayed a day and then started to drive away. But when we reached the edge of the forest, we looked at each other and, without saying a word, we turned around. We didn't want to leave. Maybe you will feel the same—or maybe not. You can open yourself to the possibility, but you can't make it happen.

To explore the Forêt de Brocéliande you will need a car, walking shoes, and a map. The tourist office in the town of Paimpont, deep in the forest, provides a detailed brochure describing a driving circuit. The tourist offices outside Mauron and in Tréhorenteuc also provide excellent information. Pick up a topo map as well, perhaps the IGN 3615 "Plein-Air - Ille et Vilaine - Randonées en Haute Bretagne - Brocéliande" or the PR (Promenade & Randonnée) "TopoGuides Brocéliande à pied" (ISBN 978-2-7514-0298-2). Plan to spend several days (a week would not be enough!), steeping yourself in the magic of Brocéliande.

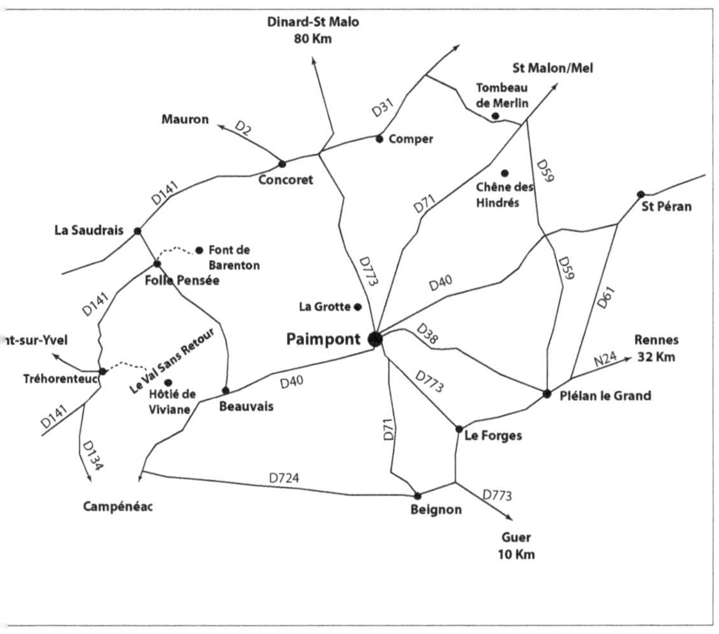

Some powerful places in the Forêt de Brocéliande

Elyn Aviva

Abbaye de Paimpont

Grotte de Notre Dame de Paimpont (Grotto of Our Lady of Paimpont)

We came upon Brocéliande by chance, taking a detour off the N24 that goes on a diagonal between Carnac and Mt St-Michel. We entered into the forest, and soon we were lost. Not lost in the "directional" sense—we knew where we were. But "lost" because we had entered a thin place, a place where magic happens and connections are made—where secrets are revealed and hidden, where mystery abounds. We didn't plan to stay—in fact, we started to leave—but when we reached the boundaries of the forest we turned around, returning to the inn where we had spent the night and asked to spend another. The desk clerk smiled and gave us back our room key. "This happens often," he assured us. (Elyn)

The market town of Paimpont, in the heart of Brocéliande, sits on the boundary between Ille-et-Vilaine to the east and Morbihan to the west. But this administrative division makes no difference to the forest, which has been there much longer than governments and bureaucracy. The town itself is small and unassuming, its buildings made of dark reddish-grey schist. Stroll through the stone archway and down the single main street, past the numerous souvenir shops laden with plastic fairies; mannequins dressed up as knights in armor, Merlin, or Guinevere; medieval-fair clothing; ceramic elves and dwarves; Celtic jewelry; stones and crystals; books on Celts, the Grail, the Knights of the Roundtable—if it relates to magic, Arthurian legends, or New Ages topics, you'll find it here.

It is easy to be cynical and think there's nothing here but gimmicky merchandising, but something there is that draws this mélange of interwoven themes. And something there is that draws the tourists and seekers who come, looking for something different, something special, something magical to enter into their lives.

Window display in a shop in Paimpont

The first time we came to Paimpont, we went into one of the shops and started talking (in a mix of languages) with the Italian clerk. He said he was a Druid bard who had come to live in the Forest of Brocéliande. He gave Gary a sprig of mistletoe he had cut with golden scissors from the top of an ancient oak during the full moon. And then he said, "People want to know how to see faeries in the forest. I tell them, you have to look with the eyes of the heart." Sage advice indeed from a purveyor of tourist souvenirs!

The Italian bard is no longer in his shop, and the shop itself has changed names. But the nearby forest, the abbey of Paimpont, the abbey park, and the grotto of the apparition are still there. They are powerful places. To begin your exploration, follow the main street to the abbey and stop at the tourist office to get driving and walking maps and brochures of the area.

The Abbaye de Paimpont was founded by St Judicaël, who was born around 580. He was King of Domnonia, a Breton kingdom said to have been founded by migrants from Dumnonia in Great Britain. Judicaël alternated between governing Domnonia and retreating to a monastery near what is now Paimpont.

In 630 he witnessed an apparition of the Virgin Mary, who asked him to build her a sanctuary. She made a spring appear on the spot—the only spring in the area with sweet-tasting water. In 645 St Judicaël built a sanctuary where the current abbey stands. Across the lake, a late-nineteenth-century grotto marks the spot of the apparition, and a statue commemorates the saint. An apparition, a spring, and a sanctuary—we've seen that combination before, at Ste-Anne d'Auray and Le Folgoët.

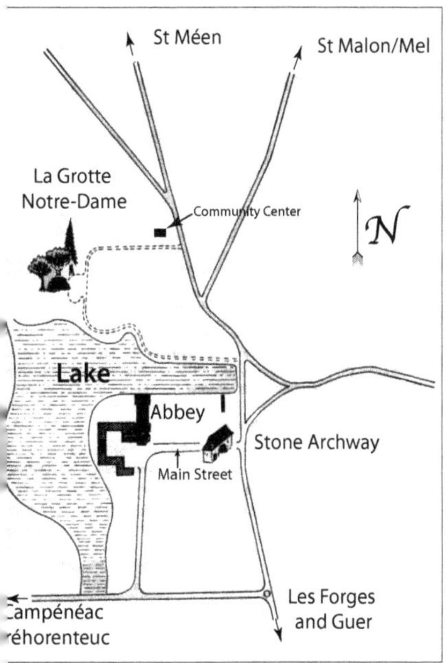

The town of Paimpont

The Vikings destroyed the original abbey in the tenth century, and another one was built to take its place. Part of the abbey was built in the twelfth to thirteenth centuries, part in the late fourteenth century, and some in later centuries. The ornate, seventeenth-century woodwork is lovely. The venerated statue of Notre Dame de Paimpont dates to the fifteenth century.

The few remaining monks were evicted during the French Revolution, and the abbey became the Paimpont parish church. Although the church has gone through numerous alterations and changes in fortune, it remains a powerful place. Stand next to the large altar and see what you sense. Gary dowsed a crossing of fire and water lines at the altar, which perhaps contributes to the palpable energy.

> "Throughout history there is a co tinuous process whereby cultu develops and changes according t the needs and prevailing beliefs the times. . . . For instance, essence personified as goddesses and go by polytheism were redefined unde monotheism as aspects of godhea e.g. angels, saints and demons. The essential natures, however, remaine unchanged. Equally, people conti ued to recognize and celebrate th inherent qualities of sacred places u der the aegis of a different theologic interpretation." Nigel Pennick, *Celt Sacred Landscapes*, p. 9.

Then stroll around the lake to the north (or drive to the community center and park). You will soon reach the abbey park. The path winds through tall trees and well-kept gardens; it follows, for a while, a babbling brook. It's a lovely place to go and be still. This area is said to have been an ancient *nemeton*, where Druids gathered to conduct ceremonies. Once again we see the re-use of sacred sites.

Elyn Aviva

The grotto

Surrounded by and topped with greenery, La Grotte

de Notre-Dame de Paimpont was constructed in 1885 after a wave of apparitions. It is a tiny replica of the grotto of Lourdes. It is built out of slag, the remains of the iron-smelting process. Behind the ornate gate are the "cave," filled with numerous plaques attesting to miracles, and a statue of the Virgin.

Elyn Aviva

The spring, statue of St. Judicaël, and grotto

Near the grotto is an imposing statue of St Judicaël, who appears to be staring still at the apparition of the Virgin. And next to the statue is an unobtrusive cavity in the earth: the spring, renowned for healing eye problems. Our local guide, Willem, told us about a miraculous healing he had witnessed at the spring. People from the area bring five-liter plastic jugs to fill with the sweet-tasting water. Clearly, this is a powerful place—and had been before the apparition, when it was sacred to the Druids.

Elyn Aviva

Trail around the lake

If you continue your walk (counterclockwise) past the grotto to the lake, you will pass a small wooden barrier. See if you notice a change of energy or temperature as you move from one location to the other. Willem told us that the park is "Christian" and that an energetic barrier at that location keeps the nature spirits out. What do you experience?

More to Experience

Most tourist brochures describe similar driving routes to reach the sites in the forest of Brocéliande. The following is a brief description of a circuit, beginning from Paimpont (though you can begin anywhere along the route). This is not intended as a substitute for a detailed map or good brochure, but it will give you a sense of the variety of evocative places in the Forêt de Brocéliande (see map on p. 115).

Leave Paimpont and drive south to the Les Forges de Paimpont, a pretty hamlet next to a lake. Its name comes from the sixteenth through nineteenth-century forges, fuelled by local iron ore, wood from the forest, and water, that were economically important to the region. Continue west to the fourteenth-century Château de Trécesson, the site of an apparition—not of the Virgin but of a White Lady. Head north to the church in Tréhorenteuc, the Val sans Retour (Valley of No Return), and the Fontaine de Barenton, described later in this guidebook (see pp. 133-153), as are several other less-visited sites (see pp. 125-131).

Near Concoret is the Château de Comper, now the Centre de l'Imaginaire Arthurien, an exhibition and research center with life-size dioramas, a large bookshop, and annual events. Comper is also the site where the faery Viviane is supposed to have been born and where she brought up Lancelot, hidden in the crystal palace that Merlin conjured in the nearby lake. The original medieval château was destroyed in the fourteenth and eighteenth centuries; the main building was restored in the nineteenth century.

Next on the circuit is the Tombeau de Merlin (Tomb of Merlin), what remains of a dynamited megalithic dolmen. The landowner was looking for buried treasure or faery gold and decided to blast the "tomb" to find it. Alas for him, alas for us.

The nearby Fontaine de Jouvence (Fountain of Youth) is a scummy spring, reached by a short walk. Once children were brought here for Druid baptism (according to the story) and the annual census, but now it is a wretched example of what loss of respect does to a place, no matter how sacred it may once have been.

If you continue east and south, you'll reach the Chêne des Hindrés, and from there you can return to Paimpont.

Willem Ordelman leads excellent private tours of well-known and less-known sites in the forest. He speaks English, among other languages, and is based at La Quinte-Essence de la Forêt de Cristal; 22 rue du Général de Gaulle, 35380 Paimpont; tel. 02 99 07 85 45; 06 80 01 19 89.

Getting There

Paimpont is about 25 miles southwest of Rennes via N24 and then D38.

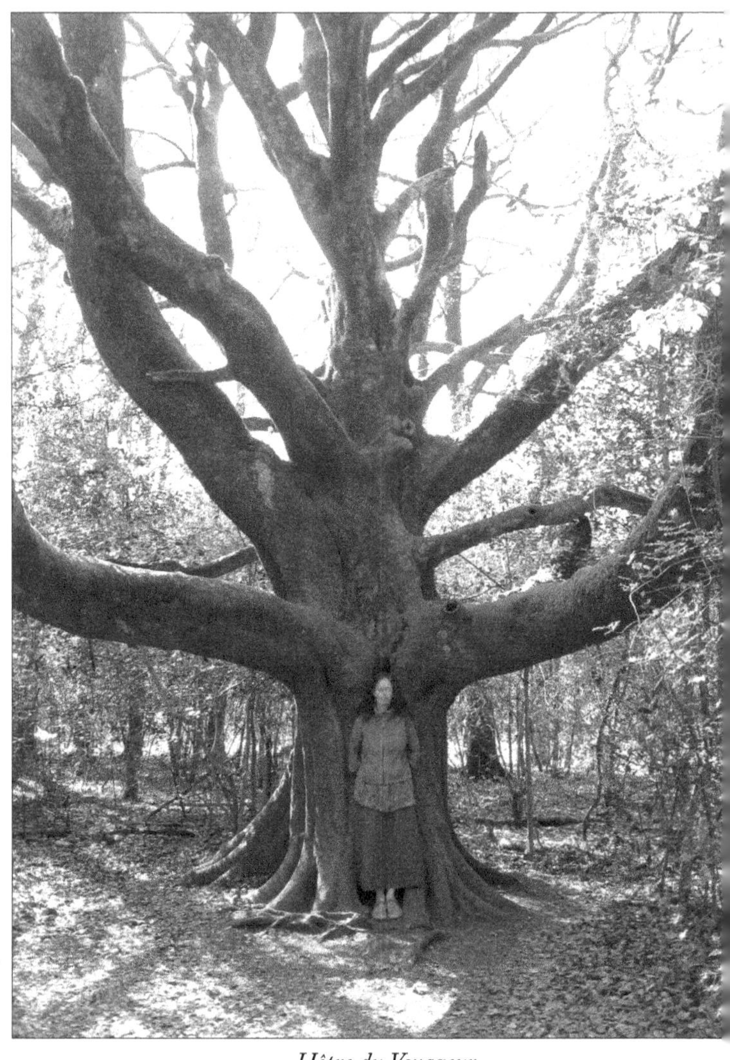
Elyn Aviva

Hêtre du Voyageur

Big Old Trees

I stand next to the ancient beech tree, the 'Grey Lady of the Woods,' admiring its graceful, outstretched branches. I remember hearing that native people say, 'We call this a beech tree,' acknowledging that 'beech tree' is not what it is, *but what we choose to call it. It is a category we impose upon a living being. I wonder what* it *calls* us*?*

'Hello,' I whisper, as if it had ears to hear. 'You are beautiful! May I come closer?' I wait a moment for a response. Slowly, I lean my back against the curvaceous trunk, resting against the smooth bark. Senses open, I smell, hear, taste, feel, and see the tree surrounding me. What, I wonder are the senses of the tree? How does it *sense* me? *(Elyn)*

The Celts considered the Forêt de Brocéliande sacred, as well as certain individual trees within the forest. With a little effort, the modern seeker can discover a number of impressive trees within the forest—impressive not just because of their size and age. Two such trees are the Chêne des Hindrés (Oak of the Damp Lands) and the Hêtre du Voyageur (Beech of the Traveler). The Celts worshipped in sacred groves called *nemetoi*. Although many of these were intentionally destroyed by conquering Romans and missionizing Christians, the remains of some *nemetoi* can still be discovered. We will visit one such place, the grove of ancient, hollow oak trees at the Chapelle de Notre-Dame de Kerneant.

In the introduction (pp. 11-13) we described the importance of trees in myth and legend. Trees represent the *axis mundi,* a link between the UnderRealm,

> "Celtic beliefs indicate that a tree ca be regarded as a deity in its own rigl and also as the seat of a deity. ... Lil human beings trees have person souls, which are manifested as sp cial qualities, strengths and medicin virtues." Nigel Pennick, *Celtic Sacr Landscapes*, p. 24.

the MiddleRealm, and the OverRealm. The roots of a tree go deep, burrowing into the dark unknown region below the surface, drawing nutrients up from the earth and stabilizing the soil. The trunk of a tree expands in the MiddleRealm or the "Green World," which humans share with the rest of the animal and plant kingdoms and the wind, the waters, the land; its leaves, through a complicated process involving sunlight and chlorophyll, take in carbon dioxide and release oxygen. No wonder so many cultures refer to the Tree of Life. The upper branches and crown of a tree extend into the sky, reaching towards heaven and the OverRealm, the realm of sun, stars, planets, and Spirit—beyond human reach. Ponder this image when you spend time interacting with the trees in the forest of Brocéliande.

When you approach a tree, do so with care and attention. See if you can feel the bands of "aura" or energy that extend out from it. Ask permission to approach, and see if you can find a place that feels a little more "open," like an entryway. Circle clockwise around the tree, gradually moving closer. If approached properly, with respect and appreciation, the tree may divulge something of its nature to you. It won't use words, but you may notice it using other means of expression. When you leave the tree, give thanks, and prepare yourself to enter back into the "other" (normative) world.

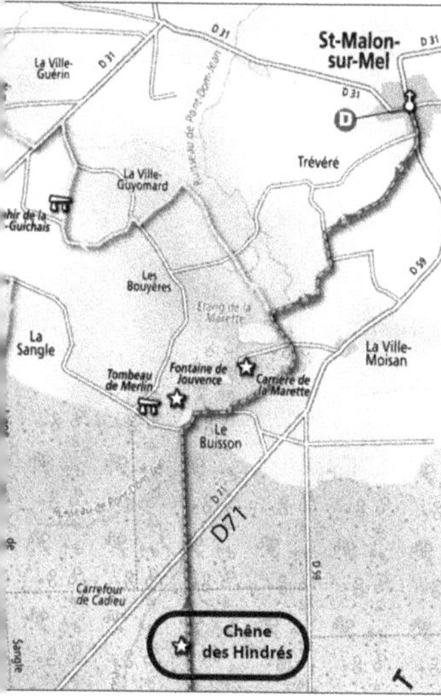

Chêne des Hindrés detailed map

Chêne des Hindrés (Oak of the Damp Lands)

This 500-year-old being of the forest is now protected by a fence—or, rather, visitors are protected from being hit by its falling branches (see cover photo). The oak tree is impressive (16.5 feet in circumference) and very old, so some of its branches can no longer bear their own weight.

Circumambulate the fence in a clockwise direction, observing the changing presentation of the oak as you walk. Pay attention to what you feel: can you sense the energy of the tree? A "presence" or "personality"? A resident dryad or "spirit"?

Elyn Aviva

The fence around the Chêne des Hindrés

We spent a lot of time with this ancient oak tree. After a while, our silent meditation was disturbed by a tour group. While the tour guide's captive audience milled around the tree, she told a heav-

Elyn Aviva

Sign at the trail head

ily Christianized version of Merlin's birth and devilish parentage. Elyn "heard" the tree expressing, "Oh my, there she goes again. Get real!" But the Chêne des Hindrés is very patient. It has been there for so long and heard so much.

At the end of her talk, the tour guide added, "This is a healing tree. People come here for healing." There was truth in that. We both felt recharged from our time with the Chêne des Hindrés.

Hêtre du Voyageur (Beech of the Traveler)

Remarkable and discreet, it hides in the forest until you stumble upon it. Maybe it seeks you out instead of you seeking it.... If you are fortunate to come upon it, walk around it clockwise, asking permission silently before approaching it more closely. Then see what it has to offer to you—or you to it. It has been here for centuries, providing respite for travelers walking through the forest (see photo on p. 124).

> "Like the Greeks, the Pag
> Celts worshipped in sac
> groves called *nemetoi.* Th
> were 'clearings open to the s
> pious enclaves set aside in wo
> land, dread places held in gr
> awe by the people, entered o
> by priests and priestesses. ...
> seems likely that, like temp
> groves were set up or dedica
> to specific deities." Nigel Penni
> *Celtic Sacred Landscapes,* p. 25.

Oak grove at the Chapelle de Notre-Dame de Kerneant

This small fifteenth-century chapel has been recently restored but was closed when we were there. Michel (of Mai-

[Ch]apelle de Notre-Dame de Kerneant

son des Sources, Tréhorenteuc) told us that the church, dedicated to Mary, is aligned with Jerusalem, not with Rome. He also said that it is energetically very powerful—in part because it is constructed of local iron-bearing stone.

Next to the chapel is a grove of ancient hollow oak trees, probably the remains of a Druid *nemeton*. Pay attention to the trees. Do you sense a difference between this grove and a random collection of trees in the forest? Do you sense a "guardian" or "spirit of the place"? Do different trees "feel" different to you? Does one (or more) attract you? Greet it with respect and ask permission to approach. We felt peaceful and calm in the circle of trees, and Gary saw branches waving though there was no breeze.

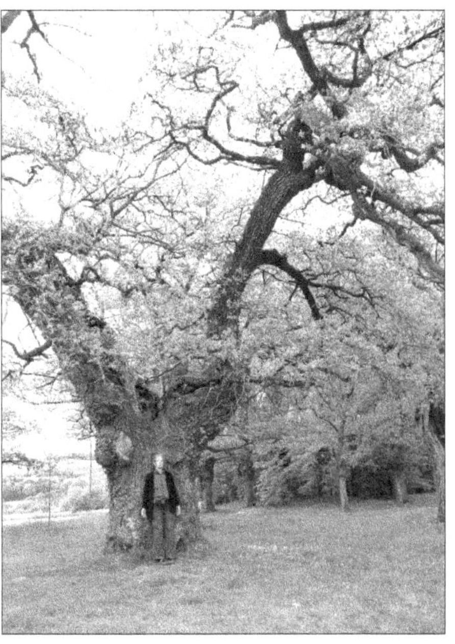

Gary White

Elyn in the nemeton

More to Experience

Other trees include le Chêne d'Anatole Le Braz; the 1000-year-old Chêne à Guillotin (33 feet in circumference) near Concoret on D141; le Hêtre de Roche Plate; and le Hêtre de Ponthus. The Beech of Ponthus is associated with Arthurian legends. According to the thirteenth-century *Romance of Ponthus,* the knight Ponthus originally came from the seaside town of Cedeira in Galicia, Spain, and was shipwrecked on the Breton coast. He fell in love with Sydoine. In order to claim her as his own, he had to undergo several tests—including conquering 50 challengers near the Fontaine de Barenton. Successful at last, they married. (Note: today, Paimpont is a sister city with Cedeira, turning ancient legend into modern relationship.) Important trees—or at least the ones with legends attached to them—are marked on some of the topo maps (see p. 115).

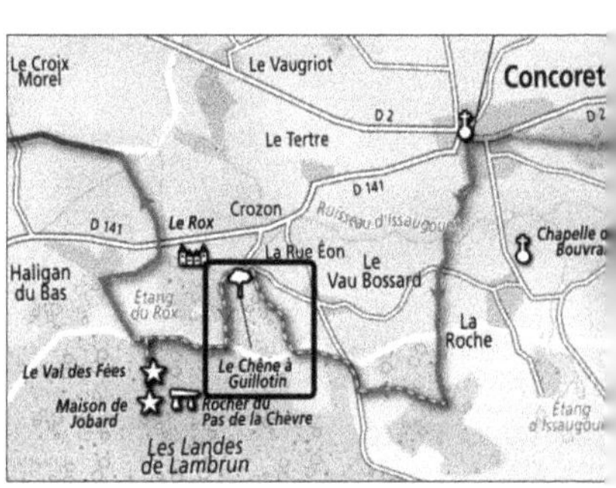

Chêne à Guillotin detailed map

Getting There

To reach the Beech of the Voyageur, go southwest from Paimpont on D40. You'll come to a pull-off on the right and a sign indicating "Private Land" and a barrier leading to a private forest road. The tree is on the left a short distance beyond the barrier.

To reach the Chêne des Hindrés from Paimpont, take D71 toward St-Malo sur Mel. You'll find the parking lot about 2 kms from the last building after the village of Telhouët (or 3.3 kms from the sign for "Telhouët" at the far edge of town). Cross the road to the wide walking trail and follow it 800 meters (half a mile) to the oak tree.

Kerneant detailed map

To reach the Chapelle de Kerneant: at Néant sur Yvet, we took the local highway 154 toward Guillar, turned right to Kerneant. Watch carefully for road signs. Additional information about the chapel can be found at http://www.morbihan-tourism.co.uk/pardon-de-notre-dame-de-kerneant/neant-sur-yvel/tabid/7747/offreid/fffedbfe-6ff4-408c-b821-0f1481f8cec6/detail-our-festivals-and-events.aspx

Notes

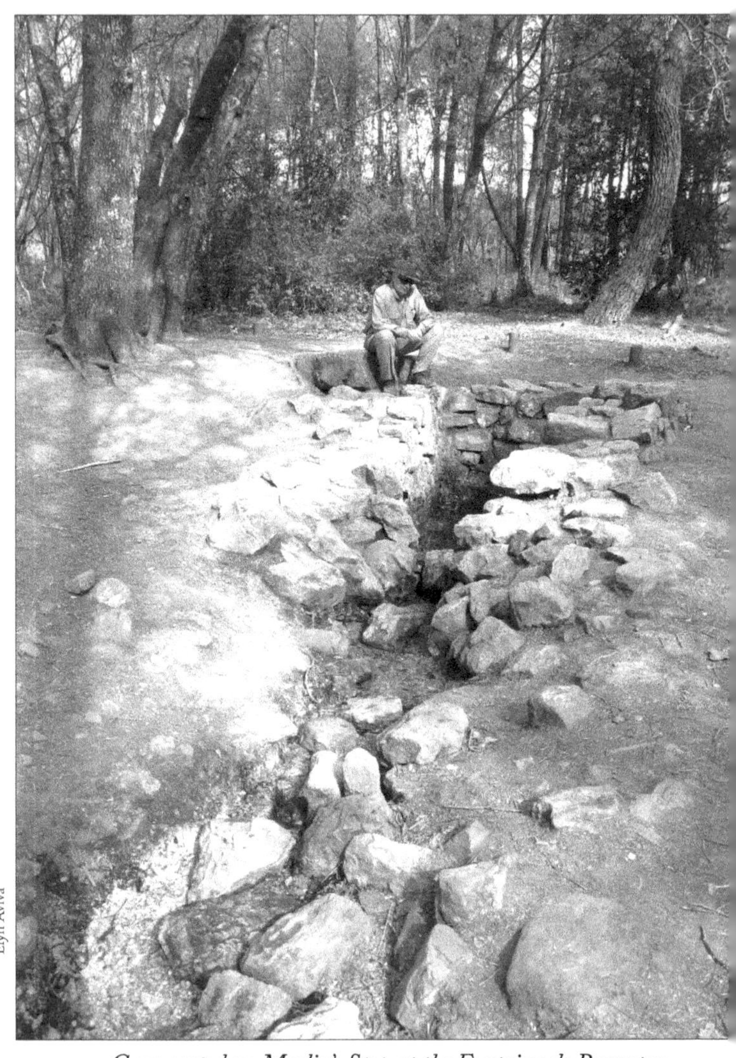
Elyn Aviva

Gary seated on Merlin's Step at the Fontaine de Barenton

Fontaine de Barenton (Barenton Fountain)

What is it about this place that generates stories of Merlin and Viviane, of weather magic, of a fierce Black Knight who guards the fountain? We stroll down the well-marked path through the forest, and I notice shifts in energy as we walk between certain boulders set on either side of the trail. Who put the stones there, and why? We reach the spring, a rock-lined cleft in the earth, in the middle of a clearing. Others have arrived before us and are perched on the edge of the fountain, staring with fascination at the bubbles that rise and burst in the waters. (Elyn)

Legends of Merlin and King Arthur abound in the Forêt de Brocéliande. One iconic location is the Fountain of Barenton, located about a mile from the parking lot at Folle Pensée, a village where (it is said) a Druidic school of medicine helped cure people with "crazy thoughts." It's possible but hard to prove. The trail meanders through the forest to the fountain where, supposedly, Merlin met Viviane—and his fate was sealed.

Surely we are in the realm of utter fantasy—or *are* we? The Arthurian cycle is a mix of real characters and fiction, of actual places embroidered with mythic stories. Merlin is mentioned in a tenth-century Latin chronicle as a prophet who overthrew the tyrant Vortigern. This Merlin helped the successor, King Amboise, rule wisely and well. Another Merlin is described by Geoffroy of Monmouth in 1135 as a powerful, prophetic king who goes mad after a devastating battle and flees to live as a wild man in the forest.

Robert de Boron describes yet another Merlin, the offspring of an innocent Christian girl raped in her sleep by a demon. This parenthood endowed the child with diabolical powers as well as great knowledge—a dangerous combination. Fortunately for all (except the demon), the child was baptized and escaped the devil's control. Christened Ambroise, the child's name changed to Merlin or Myrddin, meaning "Enchanter," and it is this Merlin who later became advisor to king Arthur. (Some scholars assert that Merlin is a title, not a person, and that there were many Merlins over the centuries, their prophecies and acts commemorated in verse.)

> "There is another pagan concept that we need to recognize if we are to regain a balanced relationship with nature: we need to recognize that nature itself has a high degree of intelligence, far higher than our own, and entirely independent of our own. This is not just a concept, that is a fact, no matter how much we may try to conceal it behind our wall of arrogance and ignorance. We try to think that we control nature; but there is no shortage of evidence that nature controls us or uses us for its own inexplicable purposes." Tom Graves, *Needles of Stone Revisited*, p. 169.

At any rate, one of these Merlins is linked with Brocéliande and the beautiful faery Viviane, daughter of King Dionas, linked with the goddess Diana, and pledged to the forest of Brocéliande. The story goes that Merlin traveled to Brittany on diplomatic duties for King Arthur. In the forest of Brocéliande he met the young Viviane at the Fontaine de Barenton. He sat on a stone beside the fountain and they fell in love. Over the years he returned regularly to the foun-

People looking at bubbles in the fountain

tain, the forest, and Viviane, instructing her in magical arts. He constructed a beautiful and invisible castle for her at the bottom of the lake at Comper; she loved the place and called herself the Lady of the Lake. She raised Lancelot there, the outstanding knight who fell in love with Arthur's queen Guinevere.

Perhaps Viviane grew weary of Merlin's frequent absences, or perhaps she wanted to keep him young—or perhaps she was a jealous, untrustworthy young faery who simply took advantage of the old, love-besotted magician. At any rate, Viviane decided to keep Merlin with her always. She tricked him into revealing the secret of how to imprison someone, and she imprisoned him in a stone or in an invisible citadel (the legends vary).

The fountain where these lovers met is the Fontaine de Barenton, and the flat stone on which Merlin sat (known as the Perron de Merlin or Merlin's Threshold) was renowned for weather magic as early as the fifth century, long before the Arthurian cycle was written. It is said that splashing a little water from the fountain onto the stone would result in fierce rainstorms. In 1835, this miraculous attribute was used to end

"We can... say that the standing ston and circles not only might have co trolled thunderstorms in the past, b that they still do to some extent. Meg lith sites are in the right places, a their shapes and semi-conductor pro erties would help the production of 'electric wind.'.... There is a correlati between megalithic sites and weath patterns—particularly of rainfall a thunderstorm activity." Tom Grav *Needles of Stone Revisited*, p. 85.

a severe drought: parish clergy came from Concoret, blessed the spring, dipped the base of a large cross in the waters and sprinkled the water on the step. According to well-documented reports, there was an immediate and highly productive thunderstorm. Subsequent efforts were also made, as late as the 1950s.

The waters of the spring bubble with nitrogen, and undoubtedly that is part of the fascination with the place. In the Middle Ages, Chrétien de Troyes wrote: "You will see the spring which bubbles/ Though its water is colder than marble." The ancient name of the fountain appears to have been Belenton, contracted from *Bel Nemeton,* a clearing sacred to the Celtic god Bel. Bel is an abbreviation of Belenos or "brilliant."

When we walked to the fountain, Elyn noticed subtle changes in energy at several locations along the trail. We noticed the locations tended to be marked by boulders on either side or once by two bent trees. Gary dowsed them and discovered strong fire lines crossing the path at those places. We felt that they were a series

Elyn Aviva

Gateway stones

> That 'something' that is manipulating oincidence would seem to be nature :self, for by getting people to build in ne right places, it ensures that those laces and structures help to maintain he harmony of nature by maintaining the flow of energies within it." Tom Graves, *Needles of Stone Revisited*, p. 170.

of "gateways," either preparing us to encounter the fountain or "protecting" the energy of the fountain in some mysterious way. Our local guide Willem concurred, saying the first gateway is as you leave the parking lot and enter the forest.

Elyn wondered whether the stones were placed there intentionally to mark the fire lines. Both Willem (see p. 123) and Michel (see p. 145) said no, that people were just "inspired" to place them there. Such inspiration is not unusual in the Forest of Brocéliande.

Getting There

From Tréhorenteuc, take D141 to Folle Pensée. Drive through the village to the parking lot. A loop trail leads to the fountain, 1.5 km (a little less than a mile) from the parking lot.

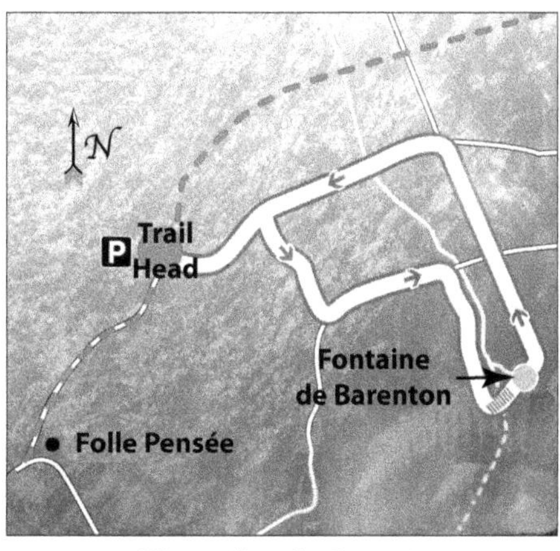

The trail to the fountain

Elyn Aviva

The Church of the Grail, Tréhorenteuc

Église de Tréhorenteuc and Fontaine de Ste- Onnen (Tréhorenteuc Church and St. Onnen's Holy Well)

"The Answer Lies Within," proclaims the carving over the south door of the small, nondescript village church. Marie, our guide, looks at us with a conspiratorial smile: "The clergy want you to think that means they have the answer—but we know that's not what it really *means." Marie thumps her chest. "The answer lies within you! It's about gnosis, not creed." Curious, we enter the old stone building. A surge of energy greets us, flowing up the nave. Marie whispers, "Telluric energies are strong here." Behind the altar, a stained-glass window glows with brilliant purples and greens. It shows a chalice suspended between two figures. "Jesus and Joseph of Arimathea," Marie explains. "That's one reason why we call this the Church of the Grail." I had the feeling there were other reasons as well, since hidden meanings and overlapping secrets were the norm in this strange temple in the middle of the primeval forest. (Elyn)*

This church in the Forest of Brocéliande is filled with evocative imagery and symbols, a mixture of Celtic, Christian, and Grail legends that exuberantly flow together to create something unique. For example, over the narthex is a huge mosaic of a white stag with a halo, a golden collar, and a cross around its neck, surrounded by red lions; in the center of the mosaic is the Fountain of Barenton and Merlin's seat. To interpret the mosaic you need to know local legends and Christian symbolism. A white stag (Merlin in disguise?) with a golden collar was said to live near the fountain, guarded by four red lions. The stag also

Stained-glass Grail window in church

represents Christ, and the four lions represent the Evangelists. The color red represents Christ's law of charity. And so on.

The church walls are covered with intriguing art. You'll see a copy of a print of the Round Table with an ornate golden Grail held by angels in the center; paintings of the nearby Valley of No Return and Barenton Fountain; stained-glass windows depicting the Round Table, Joseph of Arimathea, Jesus, and the Grail, and the life (and death) of Ste Onenn—and there's more. The paintings of the Stations of the Cross are said to have been inspired by sacred numbers associated with the twelve signs of the zodiac. Also worth noting are the numerals "1,618" carved over the lintel in the narthex. The number doesn't stand for the date of the church's construction: it stands for the Golden Mean or Golden Ratio, an important number in sacred geometry.

"Although some believe the grail is a miraculous chalice, it has also been described as a platter, a cauldron, a philospher's stone—or as the nearly unatttainable goal of spiritual transformation and mystical union with the Divine." Elyn Aviva

Decades ago this was just an ordi-

> ᵓlace is not passive. It interacts with ur consciousness in a dynamic way. contains its own memory of events ɪd its own mythic nature, its *genius ci* or spirit of place, which may not e visible but can be apprehended by ɪe human—and animal—interloper, ꞩpecially in the appropriate mental ate... ." Paul Devereux, *Re-Visioning ɪe Earth,* p. 88.

nary, nearly abandoned parish church in the middle of the small, isolated hamlet of Tréhorenteuc (pronounced Tray-oren-tooc). But then Abbé Henri Gillard was banished here for his excessively metaphysical views. Between 1942 and 1962 he transformed the seventeenth-century Église Ste-Onenne into a Temple of the Grail. Whatever unusual perspectives the priest brought with him, he was undoubtedly influenced by the legends of Arthur, Merlin, and the Grail that he breathed in with the air in Tréhorenteuc. The result is there for us to see and ponder: a church dedicated to the Grail.

Why here? One answer is, Arthurian legends swirl around the forest, and part of the Arthurian cycle describes the quest for the Holy Grail. One version of the story, told by Robert de Boron in *Joseph of Arimathea,* begins with Joseph of Arimathea offering his own al-

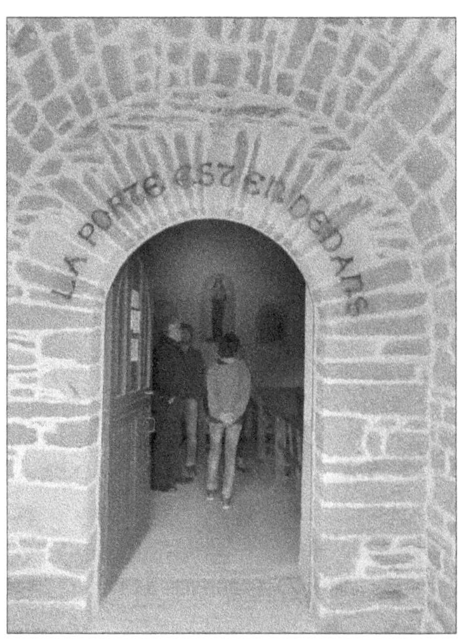

Elyn Aviva

The doorway to the church

The stag and lions mosaic

ready prepared tomb for Christ's body. When the body disappeared, the Romans accused him of stealing Christ's body and imprisoned him for many years. Christ supposedly sustained him with the Holy Grail. Eventually freed by a miracle, Joseph of Arimathea got baptized. Then he journeyed to Great Britain and founded what later became Glastonbury Abbey. Or so the story goes. At any rate, Joseph was supposedly the guardian of the Grail and established a tradition of placing the holy chalice in the center of a square table. In the sixth century, Merlin advised Arthur to change the square table into a round one. And hence, King Arthur and the Round Table. Later, King Arthur sent the knights of the Roundtable on the Quest for the Holy Grail.

Meantime, the Grail was handed down through the descendents of Joseph of Arimathea, including to one Alan (a bishop with the nickname of "Rich Fisherman") and then to his son, Josué, who was an ancestor of King Pellès, whose daughter married Lancelot of the Lake (raised by Viviane at nearby Comper). Their son, Galahad, was destined to recover the Holy Grail.

Another version of the tale states that Joseph of Arimathea buried the Grail in the forest of Brocéliande.

Fact, fiction, Celtic traditions (a bountiful cauldron is an important image in Celtic mythology) and Christian imagery, Britain and Breton—all morph together into a colorful, evocative, mysterious, and powerful church.

Fontaine de Ste-Onenn

Ste Onenn's Holy Well is located just outside of Tréhorenteuc. It is on private property and, except during the annual saint's day procession in late April, should only be visited with permission. Roger and Michel at the Maison des Sources (an excellent book, music, and art shop) have been given permission to guide people to the spring.

Roger led us to the fountain and regaled us with stories of the sixth-century Saint Onenn (also spelled Onen, Onenna, and Onenne), sister of the Breton king Judicaël (see p. 119). When she was ten years old, she had tired of her lifestyle, so she ran away to Tréhorenteuc to live with a less-noble family. Roger explained that her true name was not Onenn but "Gwenena" or Hwenena"—a diminutive of "white,"

> "At the same time there is another force or agency, which I suppose we could call 'angelic interference,' which tends to bring out-of-balance Yin and Yang into equilibrium. It is this quality which, when associated with a well, for example, makes it into a holy well, for the water of such a well will tend to re-balance the energies in people, making them whole. . . . The curative effects of 'angelic' water [e.g, Lourdes]—presumably water laden with ch'i—are well-known and well-attested...." Tom Graves, *Needles of Stone Revisited*, p. 138.

Ste Onenn's Holy Well

meaning Little White Lady in Late Gaullish, ancestor to Gallo, the language of this region of Brittany. Roger also told us that sometimes an apparition of a White Lady has been seen at the holy spring.

The entrance to the well is hidden from casual view. Trapezoidal in shape, it is a dark and mysterious slit in the earth. Stone steps lead down to a pool of spring water some ten feet below. Elyn stepped over the low upright threshold stone and walked partway down the steps. And there she sat, sheltered on three sides by the vine-draped stone supporting walls. Suddenly she felt enormous healing energy surging through her, shaking her like a rag doll. Eventually (it could have been a few minutes or an hour) the process ended.

Why her? Why there? What combination of earth, stone, and water, of living landscape and the spirit of the place, of ancient sanctity and modern need, came together at that moment, at that sacred spring? We'll never know.

> "Perhaps, after all, the Earth does harbor spirits—or there is something in the nature of certain places that can interact with the mind to produce visual imagery of a characteristic kind." Paul Devereux, *Re-Visioning the Earth,* p. 219.

The café of the Maison des Sources

More to Experience

Tréhorenteuc is a gateway to the Valley of No Return (see pp. 146-153).

Getting There

Arrive in Tréhorenteuc on D141 from La Saudrais (see map on p. 115). The tourist office next to the church is excellent and the staff can provide walking maps for trails in the area.

Ask Roger or Michel at the Maison des Sources, 13 rue de Brocéliande, to guide you to Ste Onenn's holy well. By the way, the café associated with the Maison makes wonderful vegetarian quiches.

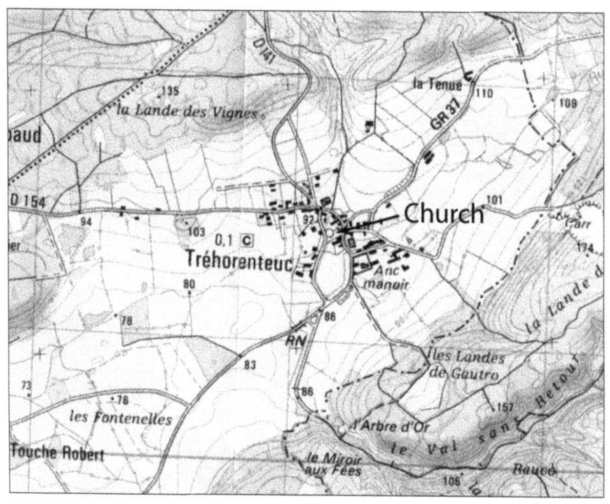

Area map

Sidney Ramsden Scott

The "Gold of Brocéliande," Val sans Retour

Val sans Retour (Valley of No Return)

We first heard about the Valley of No Return from a guide we hired to take us around Carnac. He told us that he led groups through the Valley of No Return, and he went on to describe a golden tree, the Faeries' Mirror, the House of Viviane, and a few other Arthurian-themed locations. Gary and I exchanged a look of disbelief. Who in their right mind would fall for such ludicrous claptrap? A year later we visited the Valley and realized how wrong we had been. We were enchanted by its dark forests, its streams, its ancient megaliths. Despite the fanciful names given to the various sites—or maybe because *the names evoke mythic meanings and hidden truths—these are powerful places. It is indeed difficult to leave. (Elyn)*

Just past the second car park outside of Tréhorenteuc is a pedestrian trail that leads into the Valley of No Return. Be prepared to spend a few hours—or a day—and bring a map (available from the tourist office next to the church). There is much to experience in this beautiful valley, steeped in the legends of Brocéliande. A short circuit of 4 km (2.5 miles) will take you to the Faeries' Mirror, the Tree of Gold, and the Seat of Merlin, with a splendid view over the valley. Longer treks (GR37 and variants) are also marked, but beware: it is easy to get lost in the maze of red slate valleys. Some say it's the local iron ore that makes compasses spin wildly, others that the place is enchanted.

Morgan the Faery (her name in Breton is Mor-Guen, "Whiteness of the Sea") was the daughter of the Cornish king Gorloès and half-sister to King Arthur. Her name is also spelled Morgane, Morgain,

View over the lake in Val sans Retour

Morgana, and Morgan la Fée. She may have initially been a Celtic goddess of love. Originally described as a powerful magician, trained by Merlin, celebrated for her knowledge and generosity, in later *romances* she is portrayed as a vengeful, spiteful sorceress.

The legend of the Valley of No Return tells us that Morgana became angry with her unfaithful lover Guyomart. She cast a spell over the valley so that any unfaithful knight—including him—would be unable to leave, trapped behind an invisible wall of air. From the Rocher des Faux Amants (Rock of the False Lovers), Morgana would seduce the unwary traveler. Many men passed through the valley—and many stayed. Lancelot, however, remained faithful to Queen Guinevere (though by loving Guinevere he was unfaithful to his wife, apparently a minor quibble)

Gary White

Elyn on Merlin's Seat

and was able to break the spell and free the unfaithful knights.

Following the trail from the parking lot, you enter the valley near the Faeries' Mirror pool. You are passing into the realm of myth, where things are not what they appear. Remember Viviane's crystal palace beneath the lake at Comper? Or Alice in Wonderland going through the looking glass? Near the Faeries' Mirror you'll come to the "Gold of Brocéliande," an art installation that includes a burnt chestnut tree covered with gold leaf. The artist, François Davin, created the Arbre d'Or to commemorate the disastrous fire in 1990. The conflagration burned for five days, destroying huge sections of the forest. This was the furthest spot the flames reached.

Davin wanted the golden tree to evoke the head and antlers of a stag, and it does: the great stag that ferried souls to the OtherWorld; the massive stag sometimes seen beside the Fountain of Barenton (Merlin in animal guise?); the stag associated with magic and legends; and the stag with the golden collar that represents Christ.

The sculpture carries a powerful message about the importance of protecting the forest; it represents all the forests that are destroyed for profit or by negligence. Gold is eternal, but a tree is not gold, it's alive. We can live without gold, but we can't live without trees.

The Golden Tree and the remains of five blackened trees stand together, surrounded by innumerable upright shards of Brocéliande schist (see p. 146). Miniature menhirs? Or a barrier to keep people from getting too close to the tree?

Hôtié de Viviane

If you follow the hiking trails farther into the valley, you will discover other sites, including a number of megalithic ones. The Hôtié de Viviane (Viviane's House) has been called the "Guardian of the Valley of No Return." It dates back to 2500 BCE. Also known as le Tombeau des Druides (the Tomb of the Druids), it was probably originally a rock-covered cairn, topped with earth. It faces more or less east–west. Gary dowsed a water line going down the center, crossing with a fire line near the eastern edge. This is a pattern we've seen in many churches, where a water line runs down the nave and a fire line crosses it at the transept or before the altar.

A short walk from Viviane's House but hidden in the gorse, is an outcrop of local schist that resembles a dragon's spine. Since we are in the land of magic and myth, perhaps it really *is* a dragon's spine. If you find it, sit astride the dragon's back and see what you feel. The view is outstanding.

Elyn Aviva

The Dragon's Spine

As we wandered through the Valley of No Return, Elyn

ı a personal sense, sacred sites can be ırrors that pick up your flaws, amfy them, and then throw them back you in a way that forces you to do mething about those flaws or go inne." Tom Graves, *Needles of Stone Reited*, p. 125.

pondered why stories of faithless lovers and revenge were associated with this valley. You can say they're legends, but why are they focused on this valley instead of somewhere else? Is there something about the energies in this valley that attracts that kind of legend instead of some other kind? The Valley of No Return is a good reminder that not all powerful places emanate "positive" or benign energies. We enjoyed spending time in the valley, but we suggest you pay attention to how you feel. Do uncomfortable issues arise?

More to Experience

The Jardin aux Moines (the Monks' Garden) is an unusual megalithic quadrilateral made of alternating local red schist and quartz. It is 27 meters (82 feet) long by 6 meters (20 feet) wide. It is bordered by 27 small stones on the north side and 26 on the south. The moorland around the Monks' Garden is known as the Butte aux Tombes and is dotted with small Neolithic graves. The Monks' Garden is located about 200 meters on the left off of D141 north of Tréhorenteuc.

"... I think it's safer, and more accurate, to describe sacred sites simply as power-points. They are distribution points for various energies, places that collect those energies from the overground network. Assuming a good connection between upstairs and downstairs at any given site, we can say that, crudely speaking, high ley-line density at a site will give high energy levels at that site." Tom Graves, *Needles of Stone Revisited*, p. 124.

Tertre de St-Michel

The Tertre de St-Michel (literally, the Hillock of Saint Michael) is crowned with an impressive cross-shaped menhir (the cross is a later revision) standing on a jagged stone mound in the middle of a clearing. Coming from Tréhorenteuc, drive toward Néant sur Yvet on D154. Once in town, the road curves around a tree-encircled rise on the right with a house on it. Through the trees (the remains of a *nemeton),* in the central clearing, is the Tertre de St Michel. Chapels dedicated to St Michel are often placed on top of pagan sites; here it would appear that St Michel is laying claim to both a megalith and a Druid sanctuary.

Gary dowsed a water and fire crossing at the Tertre. Standing in front of the menhir, we felt a great deal of

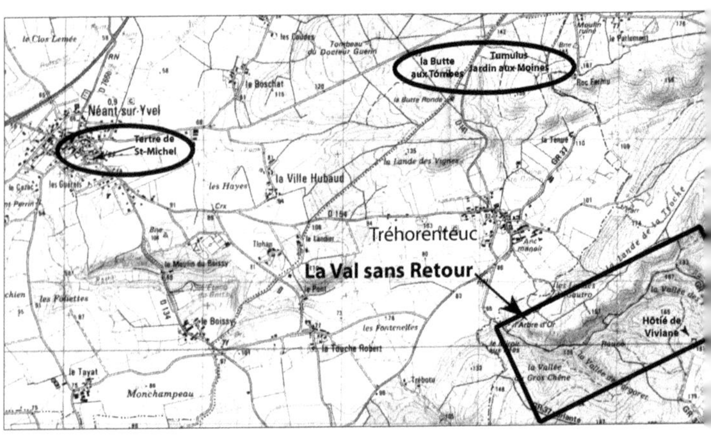

Area map

energy coming up through the ground and going out through our heads.

Getting There

The Val sans Retour begins just outside of Tréhorenteuc (see map p. 145). There is a parking lot at the trail head and no roads actually enter the valley. The IGN topo maps "Cartes de Randonnée" 1019E and 1119O cover this region in detail.

Notes

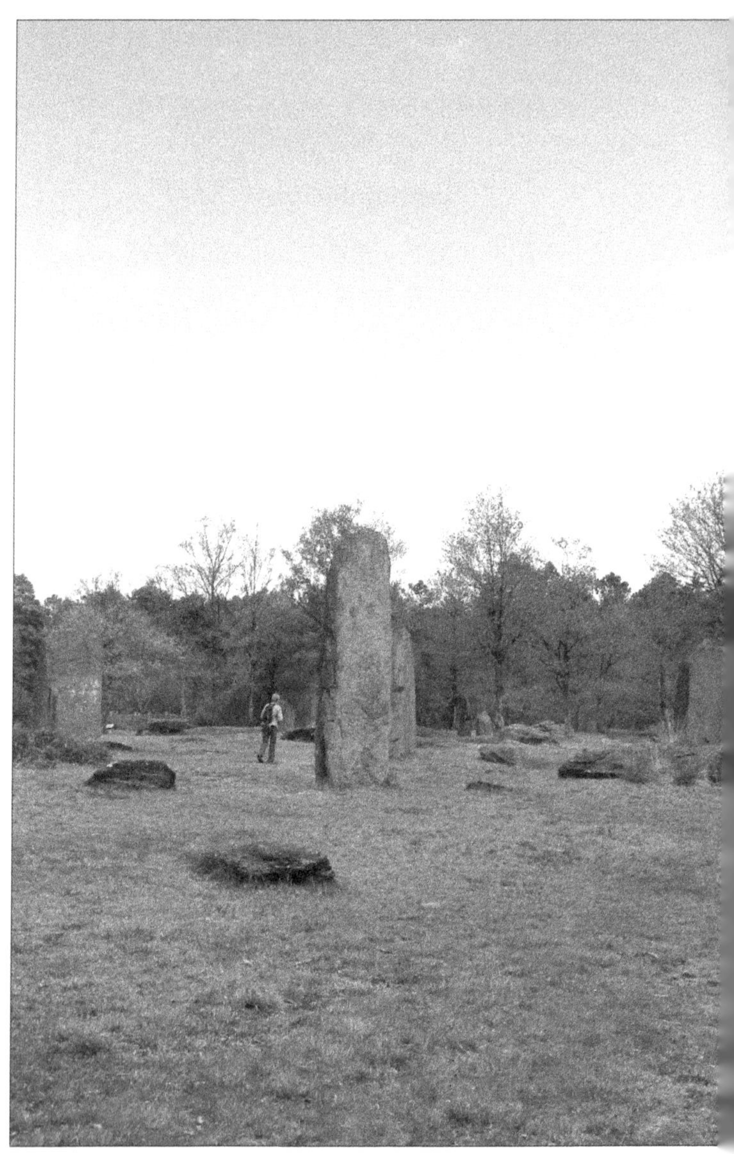
Elyn Aviva

Les Mégalithes de Monteneuf

Malestroit and Les Mégalithes de Monteneuf

Arthurian legends are enthralling, but sometimes you just want a break—a return to normalcy, or what passes for normal in this delightful region of Brittany. At least we did. So we headed out of the Forêt de Brocéliande and drove to nearby Malestroit. It's a charming 1000-year-old town, complete with a river, château, and half-timbered houses with amusing wooden sculptures. After strolling around town, enjoying the medieval ambience, we drove on to a little-known megalithic site: the Archéosite Monteneuf. We parked the car and walked across the road—and entered into a forest of ancient standing stones. (Elyn)

The Nantes-Brest Canal and the River Oust run through Malestroit, an official French "Small Town with Character," also known as the "Pearl of the Oust." It is a very welcoming town and apparently has been for quite some time, since the town's motto is "Quae numerat nummos non malestrica domus" ("Whoever counts his *bezants* [Byzantine gold coins] is not from Malestroit"). In other words, for centuries, the town has placed a great importance on being welcoming. This is, of course, good business.

Protected by a feudal moat and fortified château, in the fifteenth century Malestroit became one of the nine baronies of Brittany. In the sixteenth century, two twin locks linked Malestroit to Redon. Booming commerce helped give the town another title, "Town of the Golden Bezants."

Malestroit

Today you can walk around the small town (population 2500) and enjoy the river, the canal, a tiny island, the parks, and the medieval buildings. In the Place du Bouffay are a number of impressive sculpted granite houses. Nearby, across from St Gilles church, are fifteenth-century half-timbered houses with intriguing wooden carvings—a pig spinning, a rabbit playing Breton bagpipes, a man beating his wife, a pelican—to name a few. There is even a legend about a White Lady. With a keen eye to assisting visitors, the town has devised the Bezants Trail, a self-guided tour with numerous information boards. The route map is available from the friendly staff at the Tourist Office.

Elyn Aviva

A pig spinning wool

After strolling around Malestroit, we longed for something a bit more substantial, so we drove to the Archéosite Monteneuf (also known as the Site Mégalithique de Monteneuf or Les Pierres Droites). One of the most important megalithic sites in central Brittany, the site is located on moorland between Monteneuf

A rabbit playing bagpipes

Les Mégalithes de Monteneuf

and Guer. The extent of the site was only discovered some 25-30 years ago after a forest fire laid bare the land.

The number (420 officially listed menhirs) and size of the megaliths are impressive—as is the ability to walk among them, something it is difficult to do at Carnac. Les Pierres Droites is the name given to the alignment of menhirs, many of which are no longer upright, apparently knocked down 1000 years ago by order of the Church. Some of the menhirs are huge (one is over fifteen feet high), but others are small; in other words, there is great variety. Engineers at Coëtquidan, the nearby military college, have re-erected twenty of the menhirs in their original socket holes. In addition, there are also six *allées couvertes* (passage dolmens). Obviously, this was a very important place thousands of years ago, though the purpose of the megaliths is not really understood.

Most of the megaliths are local dark-red schist, but some are white quartz, brought from a distance. Why did the megalith builders want to use quartz? Because of its piezo-

Elyn Aviva

Sign for the Archéosite Monteneuf

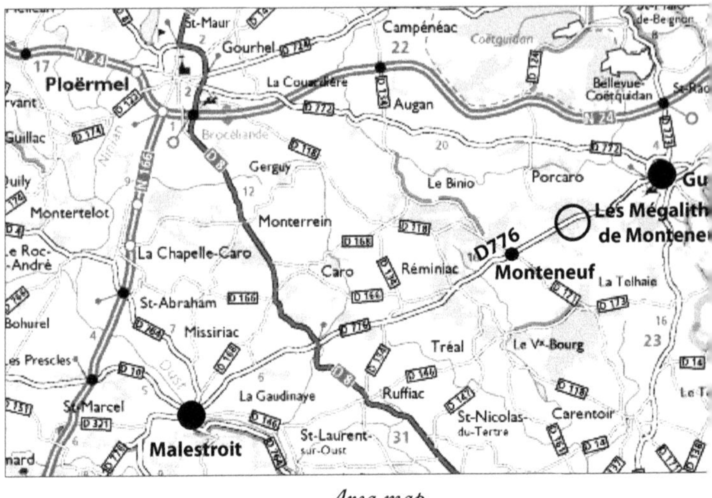

Area map

electric qualities? Because it glitters in the sun and moonlight? Spend time with the different stones and see what you experience. Do you sense a difference between the schist and the quartz?

Extensive excavations are underway, and numerous interpretive plaques describe how the menhirs were excavated and raised in Neolithic times 5500 years ago. The Archéosite includes a reconstructed Neolithic village and (when open) flint-knapping, pottery, and fiber workshops. Two walking itineraries lead to a number of interesting megaliths. Although each is over four miles in length, shorter routes are available.

Monteneuf is far enough off the beaten tourist track, and difficult enough to learn about, that we had the site almost to ourselves. It was peaceful and calm—and very evocative, even though we knew that some of the menhirs had been re-erected and the plaques turned some of the stones into exhibits. But nothing destroyed our sense that we were privileged to be there, walking among the stones.

Monteneuf doesn't have the expansiveness of Carnac, with kilometers of alignments, or the amazing carvings of Gavrinis—but it has its own special quality of abundance. Spend an afternoon, a day, among the stones and see what you experience.

More to Experience

The tenth-century chapel of St Etienne, with sixth-century foundations, is the oldest chapel in Morbihan. It is four km west of Guer. A classified historical monument, it may have been constructed over a Roman temple. At any rate, it is constructed with Gallo-Roman materials. The fifteenth-century murals are impressive. As of August 2010, it is undergoing restoration.

Getting There

Malestroit: Take D38 from Paimpont to Plélan-le-Grand. Turn on N24 in the direction of Ploërmel. Go south on D773 to Guer and take D776 to Malestroit. Detailed information can be found at www.malestroit.com.

Archéosite Monteneuf is between Guer and Malestroit on D776. You will see it near Monteneuf (before the town if you are coming from Guer). There are excellent road signs. Get detailed information at www.centreleslandes.com or www.cc-paysdeguer.fr or www.guer-coetquidan-tourisme.com or pierres.droite@gmail.com or call +33 02.97.93.26.74.

Information about Chapelle Ste-Etienne can be found at http://broceliande.guer-coetquidan-tourisme.com/spip.php?article15; call +33 02.97.93.20.23.

Elyn Aviva

Chapelle Ste-Agathe

Les Demoiselles de Langon and Chapelle Ste-Agathe (The Ladies of Langon and St. Agatha Chapel), Langon

The legends of people being turned into stones suddenly seem less silly as we stare at the shining white megaliths, sparkling in the sun. Imagine a moonlit night, with the quartz-filled stones glowing and dancing under the glittering stars.... Imagine. Just imagine.... (Elyn)

Low and lumpy, the thirty-odd menhirs called Les Demoiselles de Langon seem scattered at random across the field. Made of white quartz and quartzite schist, they were originally arranged in alignments, but time (and urban development) has not treated them well. Nonetheless, this megalithic site manages, against all expectation, to be a powerful place. The stones practically buzzed beneath our hands.

As usual, the story goes that people (in this case, a group of girls) were dancing on the heath instead of attending vespers. To punish them for their sins, they were turned into stone. (It's never clear who does the punishing, but we can imagine.) Some variant of this legend is frequently associated with standing stones—sometimes it's ladies, sometimes it's misbehaving monks, sometimes it's Roman soldiers (at Carnac), petrified "in the act."

It's easy to see simulacra—faces, human forms—in the stones and to "anthropomorphize" them, but we wonder if there isn't more to the legend than that. Perhaps the legend recalls a time, long ago, when people danced around the stones. Or perhaps it expresses the sense that the stones are (or were) "alive," vibrant with energy and even "personality." Or perhaps it is a reminder that millennia after the stones were erected, this place was sacred to the Goddess, and her priestesses conducted ceremonies here.

Les Demoiselles de Langon

The idea that there were pagan priestesses in the area is not far-fetched. Langon is home to a very intriguing chapel, Chapelle Ste-Agathe. The building began as a Gallo-Roman *thermes* (thermal baths), and it contains paintings from the second and third centuries. The paintings, visible behind the altar, are of Venus, the Goddess of Love, rising from the waves and of Eros astride a dolphin. They were discovered in 1839 during restoration of the sanctuary. The frescoes have been cited by the Celtic scholar Jean Markale as evidence that the original building was a sanctuary to Venus. Other researchers think it was an attractively decorated *thermes* and the sanctuary would have been elsewhere. At any rate, scholars agree there was worship of Venus in

Elyn Aviva

A white quartz menhir

> ring the entire Gallo-Roman od, the worship of Venus was important throughout Gaul, s made evident by the mul- statues and countless statu- s of ceramic, mass-produced he great pottery centers." Jean rkale, *The Great Goddess*, p. 93.

the area, brought by the Romans. This is simply more evidence. (Also see Vénus de Quinipily, p. 83.)

When the first Christians arrived in the region of Langon around the fifth and sixth centuries, they decided that the Roman *thermes* was a perfect site for their church. The chapel as we now see it was constructed at different times, utilizing the original Gallo-Roman construction, beginning in the sixth to seventh centuries, continuing in the ninth, and completing in the eleventh to twelfth centuries.

> "Sacred sites often take their name from the divinity that is honored there. We have seen this in the case of Bellême and Sulim, as we will see it subsequently with the many appellations given to 'Our Lady,' and to all the saints—sanctified or not—of Christianity. And even if all representations of the divinity disappear, the names maintain its memory." Jean Markale, *The Great Goddess*, p. 95.

Curiously, in 838 the name of the church was "Sancti Veneris" (Saint Venus). Apparently, Venus had been granted sainthood. One authority states that this is an outstanding example of the assimilation of the name of a goddess of the Roman pantheon by the new Christian religion, undoubtedly with the aim of gently converting the local populations. The chapel was dedicated to Ste Agathe in the seventeenth or eighteenth century. Ste Agathe was martyred by having her breasts cut off; she became the patron of nursing mothers.

Unfortunately, it is difficult to gain access to the chapel. We had to content ourselves with walking around the intriguing tiny building. From the outside, Gary dowsed a water line going up the nave and intersecting with several fire lines.

Striped pattern in the stones of Chapel Ste-Agathe

More to Experience

Near Langon are the Mégalithes de Saint-Just, also known as the Site Mégalithique des Landes de Cojoux. It is only in the last few decades that this site has been investigated in depth, and archeological work is continuing. In summer a number of walking tours are offered, some led by archeologists.

Elyn Aviva

Mégalithes de Saint-Just

The megaliths range from alignments to standing stones to dolmens to gallery graves, many accessible by following well-marked trails. Many of them are intervisible—or would be, if there wasn't so much gorse. The megaliths (starting with the alignments) were constructed from 4600 BCE to 1500 BCE, beginning in the Neolithic and ending in the Bronze Age. During the Bronze Age, many of the earlier sites were reutilized. For example, Le Château Bû was originally constructed as a dolmen in 3500 BCE; in the Bronze Age, large blocks of quartz were added, along with burials in wood. Long after their original builders had disappeared, and long after the original purposes were forgotten, the megaliths were still considered powerful places. Additional information is available at www.landes-

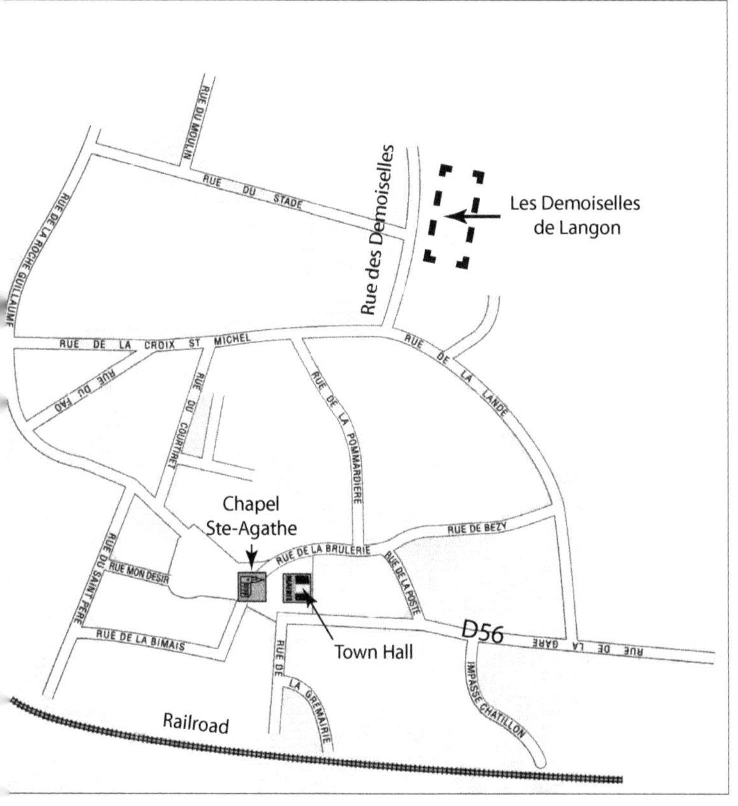

The town of Langon

de-cojoux.com. IGN topo maps 1120E and 1120O will help you explore the area.

Sign pointing to Les Demoiselles

Getting There

Come into Langon on D56. In the downtown area take Rue de la Lande to the north. Turn onto Rue des Demoiselles. You'll see a little sign pointing towards Les Demoiselles de Langon (see photos on this page). They are in the field on the right at the top of the hill.

Chapelle Ste-Agathe is near the Mairie (Town Hall) and the church. It is open as part of a guided tour (perhaps in English) in July and August. To gain access at other times, call the Mairie far in advance to schedule a guide. Be prepared to speak French. +33 02 99 087 655.

Elyn Aviva

Street sign for Rue des Demoiselles

To reach St-Just, take D177 between Redon and Rennes. St-Just is just off the highway 12.5 miles north of Redon and 30 miles south of Rennes. To reach the Site Mégalithique des Landes de Cojoux, pick up a map at the Maison Nature et Mégalithes in St-Just. Unless you want to take a very long walk, it is preferable to drive. Take D54 out of town in the direction of Camas and la Forgerais. At Camas, you'll see a sign to "Sites Mégalithiques." (Note: the map we were given shows the parking lot to the south of the Croix Madame but when we were there the parking lot had been moved to an area north and east.) An online map is available at http://www.multimap.com/maps/?zoom=16&countryCode=FR&lat=47.7656&lon=-1.9743.

Notes

Elyn Aviva

Entrance to La Roche aux Fées

Dolmen de la Roche-aux-Fées (Dolmen of the Fairies' Rock)

It's big. Very big. It's 64 feet long, built on a (relatively) high point in the (relatively) flat countryside. It's big. And it's older than the pyramids of Egypt. A huge lintel marks the entranceway, announcing that this is an important monument. We humbly bow our heads to enter this so-called "passage tomb." Soon the low corrider opens onto a spacious central chamber. It is a powerful place—but not of death. It was a council chambers, a gathering place for tribunals and justice. How do we know? I don't know how we know but we do, or at least we think we do. It's as if the stones are telling us. Long gone and long forgotten the judgments passed, the decrees declared, but the stones remember and whisper to those who have the ears to hear and take the time to listen. (Elyn)

The legend goes that in order to prove their existence to humans, faeries constructed La Roche aux Fées in one night, carrying the stones in their aprons and dropping a few as they flew. They oriented it so that, in the cold of winter, the first rays of the rising sun would warm those buried there. Whatever the truth behind the legend, the entrance to La Roche aux Fées faces the winter solstice sunrise.

Another legend recounts that the faery Viviane (whom we met in Brocéliande) constructed La Roche aux Fées. Another faery, Carabosse, was jealous of this magnificent construction and cursed all those who seek to know the number of stones in the monument. Lovers in quest of a happy marriage are protected if they count the same number of stones; or if the difference is less than two, they will marry within the year.

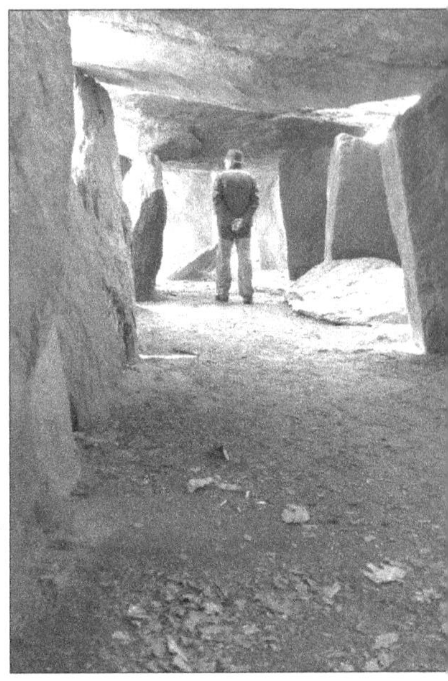

Interior of la Roche aux Fées

Another legend relates that St Armel liberated the region from a dragon that was hiding under the Fairy Rock. (The dragon is often a "stand-in" for telluric energies; it may also represent the Earth-centered religions, "conquered" by Christianity.)

The Roche aux Fées is said to be the finest dolmen in Brittany, a high point in fourth-millennium megalithic construction, and one of the largest in Europe, measuring 64 feet in length. Built sometime between 4000-3000 BCE, towards the end of the Neolithic period, it may have been used for burials but its function was not limited to that, according to a number of sources—not just us.

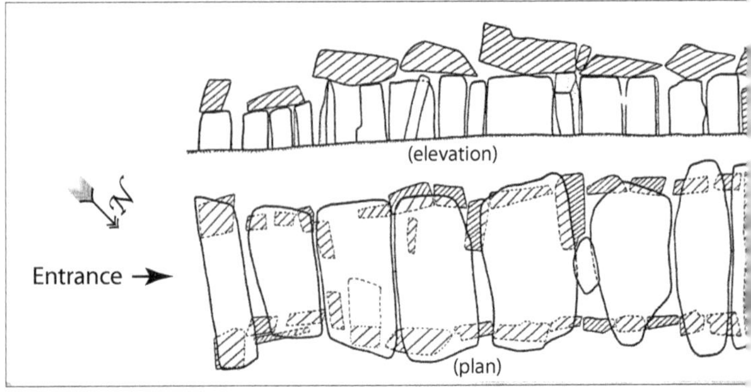

Plan of la Roche aux Fées

The purple schist dolmen was originally covered with an earthen barrow, which disappeared long ago. The stones were brought from a rock bed three miles away. Some of these blocks weigh 40 tons each, so this was a major engineering feat for humans, even if it might have been an easy task for faeries! Apparently, it was very important to move the stones to this particular location, on a little rise in a relatively flat region.

Eighteenth-century lithograph of La Roche aux Fées

Although La Roche aux Fées was known about for centuries, it was in an abandoned state until fairly recently, surrounded by vegetation and nearly inaccessible. With the encouragement of the local priest, the community decided to make it more presentable. They cleared the area and built a parking lot and a visitors' center. We don't know whether the priest was motivated by a deep connection with the dolmen or by a desire to bring more tourism to the community. Today La Roche aux Fées is presented like a jewel, showcased in the middle of a field, surrounded by oak trees.

La Roche aux Fées has an imposing entryway, an antechamber, and a spacious principle chamber. The dolmen gets higher as you move from the entry to the

Another view

back. The trilithon entryway is spectacular, formed from three large dressed stone blocks. The two massive pillars on each side are 3.3 feet by 3.3 feet and 4.3 feet high; they support a great lintel that is 18 feet long, 4.3 feet wide, and 4 feet high. You have to bend over to enter, but that only makes the principle chamber feel more impressive. The interior of the antechamber is 10 feet long, 10 feet wide, and 4 feet high. The interior of the principle chamber is 47 feet long, 13 feet wide, and 6.5 feet high. The capstones over the main chamber range in weight from 30-45 tons. In other words, it's big. And impressive. The main chamber is divided into four sections by means of three internal support slabs. We wondered if these represented "assigned" spaces for different tribal leaders or important ritual personages.

The megalith is oriented ESE, with the entryway facing the winter solstice sunrise. Although we don't really know why the Roche aux Fées was constructed, it is clear that at least part of its function had to do with marking the solar cycle. The winter solstice sunrise is very important to people who are connected to nature. It is the shortest day of the year and the beginning of the "return" of the sun, heralding the eventual coming of spring. We had the powerful feeling that this massive construction was an important council